THE
PARABLES
OF JESUS

THE PARABLES OF JESUS

RED LETTER EDITION

THE JESUS SEMINAR

ROBERT W. FUNK
BERNARD BRANDON SCOTT
JAMES R. BUTTS

SONOMA, CALIFORNIA

The cover illustrates the ancient Greek custom of using stones to cast secret ballots. In procedures such as ostracism, Greek citizens dropped stones or shards into a ceramic jar. This classical tradition provides a fitting precedent for the balloting of the Jesus Seminar.

Copyright © 1988 Polebridge Press

Library of Congress Cataloging-in-Publication Data

Funk, Robert Walter, 1926–
  The parables of Jesus.

  Bibliography: p.
  1. Jesus Christ—Parables. I. Scott, Bernard Brandon, 1941– . II. Butts, James R., 1953– .
III. Title.
BT375.2.F86 1988   226'.80663   88-25521
ISBN 0-944344-07-0 (pbk.)

10   9   8   7   6   5   4   3

Contents

Figures

$\mathcal{A}$cknowledgments

The Jesus Seminar wishes to acknowledge the devoted service of its tellers, who painstakingly collected and counted beads and ballots at each Seminar meeting. They include: Carol Ford, Jim Johnson, Stephanie Funk, Milfred Smith.

Professor James Hester of the University of Redlands provided the Seminar with computer analyses of the voting on each occasion. His help in identifying the consensus has been invaluable.

The Seminar has been dependent on its reporters for the detailed accounts of each session published in the *Forum*. The reporters include: Robert W. Funk, James R. Butts, Marcus Borg, Roy W. Hoover, and Edward F. Beutner.

The Fellows and Associates of the Jesus Seminar are also indebted to the following institutions for material assistance in hosting meetings:

Pacific School of Religion
St. Meinrad Seminary
University of Redlands
University of Notre Dame
Willamette University
Luther Northwestern Theological Seminary

The Parables of Jesus: Red Letter Edition is a collaborative effort. Bernard Brandon Scott drafted the "Introduction" and "Notes," with the assistance of Robert W. Funk. Dr. Funk provided "The Story of the Seminar" and "The Consensus." Several of the appendices are the work of James R. Butts, who also edited the whole.

Several Fellows and Associates read parts of the manuscript and offered suggestions for improvement: J. Dominic Crossan, Carol Ford, Sanford Lowe, Roy Hoover, Milfred Smith, and Hal Taussig.

The authors and editors thank the more than one hundred Fellows and Associates who devoted three years to the creation of this critical edition of the parables of Jesus.

The Origin of
Red Letter Editions

According to Laurence S. Heely, Jr., publisher of the *Christian Herald*, the idea of a red letter edition originated with Louis Klopsch around the turn of the century.

Mr. Klopsch was born in Germany in 1852 and was brought to America in 1854. He studied journalism at Columbia University. He worked his way up from stock boy to publisher of the American edition of the *Christian Herald*.

The idea of a red letter edition struck Klopsch as he read the words of Luke 22:20: "This cup is the new testament in my blood, which is shed for you." The sentence that provided the name for the second major division of the Bible—the New Testament—also offered Klopsch the idea for printing the words of Jesus in the color of his blood.

The publisher invited scholars in America and Europe "to submit passages they regarded as spoken by Christ while on earth." He thus convened the first Jesus Seminar and produced the first critical red letter edition.

Publishers subsequently abandoned the original limitation—words spoken by Jesus while on earth—and expanded the red sections to all words attributed to Jesus, while on earth, when appearing in visions, as resurrected. Indeed, the Red Letter Edition that supplied much of the information in this note (*The Open Bible*, published by Thomas Nelson, 1975) includes all words attributed to Jesus in whatever state. An edition of the *Revised Standard Version*, publication date unknown, excludes words attributed to Jesus in the Book of Revelation, but includes words spoken to Paul in his visions (for example, Acts 22:6–21). This version was published and copyrighted by World Bible Publishers, Iowa Falls, Iowa. In this instance, as in the case of *The Open Bible*, the publishers do not tell the reader who made the decision to print what in red.

Mr. Klopsch and the twentieth century were anticipated, however, by a fourteenth-century manuscript of the four gospels written in Greek and Latin. In this manuscript, the narrative text is written in vermilion, whereas the words of Jesus, the genealogy of Jesus, and the words of angels are written in crimson. Words of the disciples, of Zechariah, Elizabeth, Mary, Simeon, and John the Baptist appear in blue; the words of the Pharisees, the centurion, Judas Iscariot, and the devil are in black. The idea for a red letter edition had already occurred to some scribe 500 years earlier.

This remarkable copy of the gospels is known as Codex 16 and is housed in the Bibliothèque Nationale in Paris.

The Story of
the Jesus Seminar

Ten O'Clock Scholars

The scene is a group of academics seated around a huge U-shaped conference table. They are gospel specialists. They teach at leading colleges, universities, and seminaries in the U.S. and Canada. They represent every major Christian denomination and tradition. Jewish scholarship is also represented. They are passing small covered boxes from hand to hand, into which they are dropping red, pink, gray, and black beads through a small hole in the top. The tally of the beads will determine the color in which the parable of the Unmerciful Servant in Matthew 18:23–34 will be printed in *The Parables of Jesus: Red Letter Edition,* and in *Five Gospels: Red Letter Edition.* (It will be pink.)

Some critics quickly labelled the scene blasphemous. Other detractors joked about determining the truth by democratic vote. But the Fellows of the Jesus Seminar are undeterred. They are certain of the merits of the project. They do not think for a moment that they will determine historical truth by vote, nor are they tampering with the word of God, as some fundamentalists claim. Their purpose is elementary: They want to learn whether a scholarly consensus exists on what Jesus really said, and they want to report the results of their deliberations to a broad public in some relatively simple, lucid form.

The Jesus Seminar is the place of their joint deliberations and *Five Gospels: Red Letter Edition* the form of their final report. Interim reports will be issued on the parables (this volume), the aphorisms, and the dialogues and stories.

This is the story of how it all came about.

King James and Bible Scholars

A King James Bible bound in black, imitation leather, with gilt edges, was the coffee table centerpiece of the home of my youth. In that sacrosanct volume, the words of Jesus were printed in red. It was a red letter edition. Many years later I was to come back to that simple and omnipresent version of the Bible that has had such profound influence on the shaping of what Americans think about the Bible. Meanwhile, it was not long before I learned that the Bible scholars working for King James had very limited tools and severely restricted knowledge: the King James version rested on inferior Hebrew and Greek manuscripts and the translators had little knowledge of the ancient world. In addition, the English its translators wrote and spoke has since become archaic.

In the University I attended, one of my instructors taught me that scholars have been studying the gospels using the scientific methods of modern critical scholarship for more than two hundred years. I soon learned the difference between a literalist view of the text and a critical approach. A literalist insists that everything written in the scriptures is literally true or it is not true at all. A critical scholar is one whose conclusions are determined, not by prior religious convictions, but by the evidence. As in the case of many other students, my naive piety was no match for the facts. I came to see that Jesus, like many other sages in the ancient world, became a repository of common lore in a predominantly oral culture. Although I didn't know it then, a critical red letter edition lay way off in my future.

I have been a student of the gospels for more than forty years. I am acutely aware that longevity, or even piety, does not necessarily mean competence. No amount of service, or good will, or even devotion, can substitute for proper training, extensive learning, and tough peer review. Like all other students who aspired to join the professional guild of critical scholars, I was required to pass through years of rigorous training, four academic degrees, and endless papers and dissertations. Along the way I had to master more than one ancient language, along with a few modern languages and a vast array of secondary literature in those tongues. I mention these details because many Americans are unaware of what a proper education in the field of biblical studies entails.

Yet examinations were not over when I finished seminary and graduate school. As a working scholar in the field of biblical studies, I was obliged to put my ideas, my translations, my interpretations, my theories, into the public domain of scholarship by means of essays and books. The examinations got tougher, rather than easier, as time went by. My professional colleagues were tough on me: they corrected, chided, counseled— and encouraged. Occasionally I was rewarded with applause and approval. This is the way of critical scholarship: propose, review, reformulate, publish, test, test, test. A half-dozen books and more than one hundred articles later, I am still forced to run the gauntlet of criticism each time I open my mouth or turn on my computer.

The mills of scholarship grind slowly, but they grind exceedingly small. I have been subject to no small amount of grinding.

The end product of this process is something called the scholarly consensus. Every scholar aspires to contribute to that consensus and to become a representative of it.

After thirty-three years in the classroom—college, seminary, graduate school—I decided to embark on the great venture and write a book on Jesus. It is the ambition of many who have spent their lives investigating the gospels. I thought I would endeavor to sum up everything I have learned about Jesus from my colleagues, past and present, and from my own research. I wanted to contribute in some small way to the modification of the existing scholarly consensus and yet affirm its dominant direction. This modest resolve was to lead me in surprising new directions and to open challenging and exciting vistas. In academic life one should never be too old to learn.

Here is what happened.

The Cupboard was Bare

The first step was to compile a list of the things Jesus said and the things he did. A raw list would then of course have to be refined in the light of the history of gospel scholarship and a new, critical list created. This second list would be the data base from which I would work in writing my sketch of Jesus.

It is the way of scholarship to begin by going to the library and reviewing everything written on the subject. I hoped to find both raw and refined lists among the dusty tomes housed there. Here is where surprise and astonishment set in.

In the first instance, I could find no raw lists of words or deeds that could serve as my raw data base. So far as I have been able to discover, no one had ever compiled such a list of all the words attributed to Jesus in the first three hundred years following his death.

Astonishment began to grow when, among the many scholarly books written on Jesus in the last century and more (my beginning point was about 1880), I could find no critical list of sayings and deeds on which a particular scholar had based his or her picture of Jesus. A few partial lists turned up, but nothing exhaustive. Although scholars of the gospels regularly make the distinction between authentic and inauthentic materials, they are not in the habit of revealing the results explicitly. In quizzing contemporary colleagues, I was equally surprised to learn that no one had compiled a raw list, or worked up a critical list, of Jesus materials. This in spite of the fact that most of them lecture or write about Jesus nearly every day. I felt destiny beckoning.

The Tom Sawyer Approach to Fence Painting

When one has a picket fence to paint, the best strategy is to enlist help. I did just that. I sat down and wrote letters to thirty of my colleagues in gospel studies and invited them to join me in forming the Jesus Seminar. Eventually the membership was to grow to more than two hundred, more or less equally divided between established academic scholars (Fellows) and interested nonspecialists (Associates).

We agreed to meet twice a year. The original thirty Charter Fellows nominated additional Fellows and Associates. The membership grew. No one has ever been refused membership in the Seminar. However, one Fellow lost his academic post because of his participation, and others are unable to acknowledge publicly that they belong. In spite of these problems, the group has developed a strong sense of mission and achievement as it has pursued its agenda. It is now entering the fourth year of a five-year agenda. *The Parables of Jesus: Red Letter Edition* is its first report outside the pages of the *Forum,* the journal of the Seminar and Westar Institute, the sponsoring organization.

The aims of the Seminar were two: (1) we were to compile a raw list of all the words attributed to Jesus in the first three centuries (down to 300 C.E.). These sayings and parables were to be arranged as parallels, so that all versions of the same item would appear side by side on the page for close comparison and study. We decided to defer listing the deeds of Jesus until a second phase of the Seminar. (2) We were then to sort through this list and determine, on the basis of scholarly consensus, which items probably echoed or mirrored the voice of Jesus, and which items belong to subsequent stages of the Jesus tradition.

These aims seem simple enough. But leave it to scholars to complicate what appears to be simple and straightforward.

Heresy and Harrassment

This is the best point at which to insert warnings that should go on the label of the Jesus Seminar.

This is what I said to the original Charter Fellows in March, 1985:

> We are about to embark on a momentous enterprise. We are going to inquire simply, rigorously after the voice of Jesus, after what he really said.
>
> In this process, we will be asking a question that borders the sacred, that even abuts blasphemy, for many in our society. As a consequence, the course we shall follow may prove hazardous. We may well provoke hostility. But we will set out, in spite of the dangers, because we are professionals and because the issue of Jesus is there to be faced.

We have indeed provoked controversy and been subject to hostile attacks. But the Seminar has also attracted the attention of the news media and we have found wide and enthusiastic support.

Academic folk are a retiring lot. They like noiseless libraries and private sanctuaries for reflection. They prefer books to lectures, and solitude to public display. To this disposition, I am inspired to say: We have too long buried our considered views of Jesus and the gospels in technical jargon and in obscure journals. We have hesitated to contradict what TV evangelists and pulp religious authors have to say about the Bible for fear of political reprisal and public controversy. And the charge of popularizing or sensationalizing biblical issues is anathema to promotion and tenure committees in the institutions of higher learning where we work. It is time for us to quit the library and study and speak up.

The level of public knowledge of matters biblical borders on the illiterate. The church has failed in its historic mission to educate the public in the fourth "R," religion. Many Americans cannot even name the four canonical gospels. The public is poorly informed about any of the assured results of critical scholarship, although those results are commonly taught in colleges, universities, and seminaries. In this vacuum, drugstore books and magazines play on the fears and ignorance of the uninformed. Radio and TV evangelists indulge in platitudes and pieties. In contrast, the Jesus Seminar is a clarion call to enlightenment. It is for those who prefer facts to fancies, history to histrionics, science to superstition, where Jesus and the gospels are concerned.

Yet one should heed the warning on the label: a seventeenth century view of the Bible will not long remain intact in the face of a little knowledge. As I have frequently warned my students over the years, learning has a way of opening up new vistas and eroding uninformed opinion.

When You See White Smoke From the Chimney . . .

The Seminar made good progress in compiling the basic inventory of words attributed to Jesus. J. Dominic Crossan, a leading gospels scholar, author of numerous well-known books and essays, professor at DePaul University, took the lead in creating *Sayings Parallels.* This workbook contains more than a thousand versions of 503 items, classified in four categories: parables, aphorisms, dialogues, and stories incorporating words attributed to Jesus. It covers all intracanonical and extracanonical sources in the first three hundred years. *Sayings Parallels* became the official workbook of the Jesus Seminar.

Now the fun was to begin. We formed specific agendas of items to be reviewed and evaluated at each of our semiannual meetings. Scholarly essays were prepared and distributed in advance on each item. The meetings themselves were devoted to argument and debate. The question then became: how shall we determine whether a scholarly consensus exists on a particular item? And how shall we measure the magnitude of that consensus?

My bold suggestion was that we vote on each item. There were two reasons for so doing. First, scholars are prone to put off making decisions until they have had time for further study, or until they have read the latest article or heard the most recent argument, or just because they are trained to hold issues open to further knowledge. The essence of scholarship is attention to endless detail and the patience of Job in weighing evidence.

Caution has to be balanced with the willingness to make tough decisions, even for humanists. Knowledge of literature, or art, or the Bible, should be good for something. Yet I know academics well enough to know we will not readily come to decision unless we agree in advance to a decision-making procedure. Further, in the case of the Jesus Seminar, we needed the means to report the results of our deliberations to a broad public. But we had not decided on how that could be done. A critical red letter edition of the gospels seemed the best way to make a report readily comprehensible to the nonspecialist reader browsing in the local bookstore or library.

Voting to me was a way to ascertain whether a scholarly consensus existed. After all, committees creating critical texts of the Greek New Testament, such as the one responsible for the United Bible Societies Greek Testament, vote in the course of their deliberations about whether to print this or that text and about what to consign to variants in the notes. And translation committees, such as the one creating the *Revised Standard Version*, vote in the course of their work on which translation proposal to adopt. In so doing, they are only attempting to discover whether the members around the table agree on a point and the extent of that agreement. Of course, they do not thereby determine the ultimate truth; they only learn what the majority among them think is the truth.

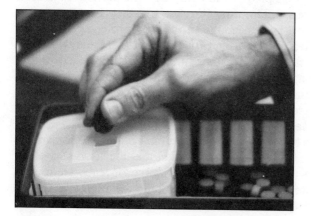

A Fellow voting at a
Jesus Seminar meeting.

Similarly, I deemed it entirely consonant with such procedures to ask members of the Jesus Seminar, after appropriate preparation and review, to decide whether, in their collective judgment, a given item did or did not permit the voice of Jesus to be heard. The old model of the red letter edition—here I go back to my childhood—suggested to me that a given item should be labelled either red (Jesus did say it or something like it) or black (he did not).

But my colleagues resisted making matters so simple. We ended by adopting four categories. In addition to red, we permitted a pink vote for those who were not quite sure of red, or thought red was too strong. And for those who did not quite want to print an item in black, we permitted a gray vote. Four colors means that our report will not be a simple red letter edition; it will be a color-coded edition in red, pink, gray, and black.

In a sense, the formation of a scholarly consensus customarily takes place by "voting," although the voting occurs covertly and over a long period of time. One scholar discovers a fact, or proposes a theory, publishes his work, and other scholars approve and adopt his work or disapprove and reject it, all normally in writing. Eventually, the body of scholars generally agrees to such proposals and a consensus is formed, or disagrees and a different proposal is advanced.

In the Jesus Seminar, as in textual and translation committees, we are merely trying to shorten the cycle by asking scholars to express their minds on specific items under consideration. Surgery committees in hospitals, with the patient lying in bed, have to decide whether to operate or not, at the time; they cannot afford to publish their opinions in the *New England Journal of Medicine* and wait for letters to the editor. It is equally appropriate, though perhaps less urgent, to ask biblical scholars to state what they think, at this point, on a given topic, particularly when that topic is of widespread public interest and concern. On a radio talk show recently, a caller asked me whether there was a hell. I responded: Do you want to know whether Jesus thought there was a hell? The caller insisted on the general question as one that troubled her deeply and immediately. She was not interested in the history of the concept; she just wanted to know whether there was one, yes or no. I gave her my answer: there is not a hell, certainly not in the mythological sense depicted in the Bible. Scholars of the Bible have the responsibility to tell the public what they know, or think they know, just as do politicians, medical experts, economists, anthropologists, chemists, ecologists, and other experts, where knowledge impinges on the public good.

My book on Jesus has been postponed. It awaits the complete reports of the Jesus Seminar. *The Aphorisms of Jesus: Red Letter Edition* and *The Dialogues and Stories of Jesus: Red Letter Edition* are due off the press in 1989. *Five Gospels: Red Letter Edition* will be ready in 1990. Then I can once again think of writing my book on Jesus.

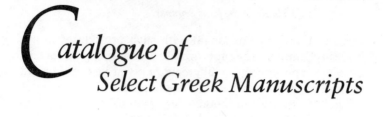

Catalogue of Select Greek Manuscripts

Listed in Chronological Order

Designation	Date	Contents	Location/Notes
Greek Papyri			
P. Egerton 2	100–150	Unknown gospel frags.	London
P52	ca. 125	John frag.	Manchester
P75	175–225	Luke & John frags.	Cologny
POxy 2949	ca. 200	Peter frags.	Oxford
POxy 1	ca. 200	Thom frag.	Oxford
POxy 655	ca. 200	Thom frag.	Cambridge, Mass.
P64 & P67	ca. 200	Matt frag.	Oxford; Barcelona
P66	ca. 200	John frags.	Cologny; Dublin
P77	II/III	Matt 23:30–39	Oxford
P1	III	Matt frags.	Philadelphia
P4	III	Luke frags.	Paris
P45	III	Gospels & Acts	Dublin
P53	III	Matt & Acts frags.	Ann Arbor, Mich.
P69	III	Luke frags.	Oxford
P70	III	Matt frags.	Oxford
P37	III/IV	Matt 26:19–52	Ann Arbor, Mich.
Greek Uncials			
א	IV	e, a, p, r	British Museum; only complete copy of Greek New Testament in unical script.
B	IV	e, a, p	Vatican Library
A	V	e, a, p, r	British Museum
C	V	e, a, p, r	Paris
D	V	e, a	Cambridge
W	V	e	Washington, D.C.
θ	IX	e	Tiflis, Georgia, USSR

Codes & Definitions:
All dates are C.E. Roman numerals indicate centuries.
Contents: e=gospels; a=Acts; p=letters; r=Revelation.
Papyrus: writing material made from Egyptian reeds.
Parchment: writing material made from animal skins.
Uncials: a form of writing using all capital letters.

Catalogue of Written Gospels

Narrative Gospels

Gospel of Matthew   An anonymous author compiled the Gospel of Matthew after the fall of Jerusalem in 70 c.e. and sometime before the Council of Jamnia, 90 c.e. This is the period when the Christian community was seeking its own identity over against Judaism, and when Judaism was attempting to recover from the loss of the center of its worship, the temple. Matthew can be dated to about 85 c.e., give or take a few years.

Matthew was composed in Greek in dependence on Greek Mark and Greek Q. It is therefore incorrect to identify it with a gospel composed in Hebrew by a disciple of Jesus.

Gospel of Mark   An anonymous author composed the Gospel of Mark shortly after the destruction of the temple in 70 c.e. Mark is responsible for forming the first chronological outline of the life of Jesus. He may also be responsible for the first connected account of Jesus' passion (Mark 14–16). He reflects the early Christian view that God was about to bring history to an end in an apocalyptic conflagration.

The Gospel of Mark is attributed to John Mark, a companion of Paul and perhaps an associate of Peter. This attribution, like others in the ancient world, is the product of speculation.

Mark became quickly established in the Christian community as indicated by the fact that Matthew and Luke made use of his text in creating their gospels a few years later.

Gospel of Luke   Luke-Acts, a two-volume work by a single author, depicts the emergence of Christianity on the world stage. It was composed around 85 c.e., during the same period as Matthew. Whereas Matthew was concerned with the Jewish reaction to Christianity, Luke is preoccupied with developments among the Gentiles.

The tradition that Luke the physician and companion of Paul was the author of Luke-Acts goes back to the second century c.e. It is improbable that the author of Luke-Acts was a physician and it is doubtful that he was a companion of Paul. As in the case of the other canonical gospels, the author is anonymous.

Gospel of John   The Gospel of John was allegedly written by John, son of Zebedee, one of an inner group of disciples. According to legend, John lived to a ripe old age in Ephesus where he composed the gospel, three letters, and possibly the Book of Revelation. The legend is highly improbable.

The Gospel of John was probably written towards the close of the first century c.e., which makes it a close contemporary of Matthew and Luke. It exhibits evidence of having gone through several editions. Many scholars therefore conclude that John is the product of a "school," which may indeed have been formed by the John of the legend.

Its place of origin is unknown. It was clearly created in a Hellenistic city of some magnitude with a strong Jewish community. A city in Asia Minor or Syria, or possibly Alexandria in Egypt, would do.

It is uncertain whether John knew the Synoptics. He almost certainly made use of a "signs" source and possibly a source consisting of lengthy discourses.

Sayings Gospels

Gospel of Thomas   The Gospel of Thomas contains 114 sayings of Jesus, consisting of wisdom sayings, parables, proverbs, and prophecies attributed to Jesus. It has virtually no narrative content.

Thomas is extant in complete form only in a Coptic translation found among the fifty-two tractates that make up the Coptic Gnostic Library discovered at Nag Hammadi, Egypt, in 1945. Three fragments of the original Greek version of Thomas were discovered at Oxyrhynchus (1, 654, 655) in Egypt around the turn of the century. The fragments can be dated to around 200 C.E.

Thomas is widely regarded as an independent witness to the sayings of Jesus, comparable in form to so-called Q, a sayings collection believed to function as one of two sources utilized by Matthew and Luke in creating their gospels.

Dialogue of the Savior   Dialogue of the Savior is a fragmentary and composite document containing dialogues of Jesus with three of his disciples, Judas, Matthew, and Miriam. It was found at Nag Hammadi, Egypt, in 1945.

The earlier portions of the dialogue may be dated to the second half of the first century C.E., while the final form of the Dialogue of the Savior is probably to be dated to the second half of the second century C.E.

Dialogue of the Savior is closely related to the Gospel of Thomas and the Gospel of John.

Apocryphon of James   Apocryphon of James is a Coptic translation of a Greek original containing a dialogue of Jesus with Peter and James. Apocryphon of James was found among the codices of the Nag Hammadi Library in Eygpt in 1945.

Apocryphon of James lacks a narrative framework; like Thomas and Q, it consists entirely of sayings, parables, prophecies, and rules governing the Christian community attributed to Jesus. It is the risen Jesus who speaks. The whole is embedded in a letter purportedly written in Hebrew by James.

Apocryphon of James was probably composed during the course of the second century C.E.

Infancy Gospels

Infancy Gospel of Thomas   Infancy Gospel of Thomas is a narrative of the miraculous works of the young magician-hero, Jesus, prior to his twelfth birthday. Infancy Gospel of Thomas continues the *divine man* tradition of the ancient world: itinerant miracle workers accredited by their amazing deeds.

Infancy Gospel of Thomas is preserved in a Syriac manuscript of the fourth century C.E. and in Greek manuscripts of the fourteenth through the sixteenth centuries C.E. The gospel is based on oral sources and the Gospel of Luke. In its original form it may be as old as the second century C.E.

Infancy Gospel of James   Infancy Gospel of James is an infancy gospel containing an account of the birth and dedication of Mary and the birth of Jesus. The traditional title *Protevangelium* indicates that the events recorded precede those narrated in the canonical gospels. Infancy James is dated in the period mid-second century C.E. to early third century C.E.

Passion Gospels

Gospel of Peter   The Gospel of Peter is preserved only as a fragment discovered in upper Egypt in 1886–1887; the language is Greek and the fragment dates to the eighth or ninth century C.E. However, two Greek papyrus fragments from Oxyrhynchus, dating to late second or early third century C.E., may also belong to the Gospel of Peter.

The Gospel of Peter contains a passion narrative, an epiphany story, an account of the empty tomb, and the beginning of a resurrection story.

In its original form, the Gospel of Peter may have arisen in the second half of the first century C.E.

Acts of Pilate   The Acts of Pilate is an elaborate account of Jesus' trial before Pontius Pilate, his crucifixion and burial, accounts of the empty tomb, and a discussion of his resurrection by a council of Jewish elders. It is an example of early Christian apologetic in narrative form.

The original Acts of Pilate was probably written in Greek sometime during the second or third century C.E. The prologue claims that it was written by Nicodemus in Hebrew shortly after Jesus' death. The Acts of Pilate was eventually incorporated into the Gospel of Nicodemus. It is preserved in several medieval Greek manuscripts.

Fragments

Oxyrhynchus Papyrus 1224   Oxyrhynchus Papyrus 1224 is the remains of a papyrus codex containing fragments of an unknown gospel. It can be dated to the beginning of the fourth century C.E.

Oxyrhynchus Papyrus 840   Oxyrhynchus Papyrus 840 is a single leaf of a Greek parchment containing fragments that can be dated to the fourth century C.E. It contains the conclusion of a discourse between Jesus and his disciples and a controversy story involving Jesus and a Pharasaic chief priest in the temple court.

Papyrus Egerton 2   A fragment of an unknown gospel dated to the beginning of the second century C.E. Papyrus Egerton 2 contains the healing of a leper, controversy over payment of taxes, miracle of Jesus on the Jordan, plus two segments closely related to the Gospel of John.

Papyrus Cairensis 10 735   Papyrus Cairensis may be a fragment of a noncanonical gospel containing the story of Jesus' birth and flight to Egypt. The fragment is dated to the sixth or seventh cenury C.E. Further identification has not been possible.

Fayyum Fragment   Fayyum Fragment is a fragment of the third century C.E. containing an excerpt from an unknown gospel. The text is too fragmentary to warrant definitive conclusions.

Freer Logion   The Freer logion is a variant reading in codex W acquired by Charles L. Freer of Detroit in 1906 and now lodged in the Freer Museum of the Smithsonian Institution in Washington, D.C. (late fourth or early fifth century C.E.). The variant in question is an insertion in the Gospel of Mark at 16:4.

Secret Gospel of Mark   Secret Mark is a fragment of an early edition of the Gospel of Mark containing a story of the raising of a young man from the dead, a rite of initiation, and an encounter of Jesus with three women in Jericho. These stories are presently embedded in a letter of Clement of Alexandria (second century C.E.), the copy of which dates to the eighteenth century C.E. Secret Mark, however, may go back in its original form to the early second C.E.

Gospel of the Ebionites   A Jewish-Christian gospel preserved only in quotations by Epiphanius (fourth century C.E.). The original title is unknown. The Ebionites were Greek-speaking Jewish Christians who flourished in the second and third centuries C.E. Their gospel, erroneously called the Hebrew Gospel by Epiphanius, probably dates to the mid-second century C.E.

Gospel of the Egyptians   The Gospel of the Egyptians consists of sayings of Jesus. The few fragments extant are preserved in Greek by Clement of Alexandria (end of the second century C.E.). The gospel appears to be oriented to sexual asceticism, to judge by the few remaining fragments. Gospel of the Egyptians arose in the period 50–150 C.E.

Gospel of the Hebrews   The Gospel of the Hebrews contains traditions of Jesus' pre-existence and coming into the world, his baptism and temptation, a few of his sayings, and an account of his resurrected appearance to James, his brother (1 Cor 15:7). The provenance of the Gospel of the Hebrews is probably Egypt. It was composed sometime between the mid-first century C.E. and mid-second century C.E. Gospel of the Hebrews has been lost except for quotations and allusions preserved by the Church Fathers.

Gospel of the Nazoreans   The Gospel of the Nazoreans is an expanded version of the Gospel of Matthew. It is preserved in quotations and allusions in the Church Fathers and in marginal notations found in a number of medieval manuscripts. These marginal notations appear to go back to a single "Zion Gospel" edition composed prior to 500 C.E. Gospel of the Nazoreans is evidently a translation into Aramaic or Syriac of Greek Matthew, with additions.

Gospel of the Nazoreans is first quoted by Hegesippus around 180 C.E. Its provenance is probably western Syria.

Introduction

What Did Jesus Really Say?

Modern Critical Scholarship

Fundamentalists and other conservatives often advance the claim that Jesus said exactly what is ascribed to him in the four gospels included in the *canon* of the New Testament. God through the Holy Spirit, they say, inspired the canonical writers, Matthew, Mark, Luke, and John, to record exactly what Jesus taught and did, nothing more, nothing less. Other gospels, like the newly discovered Gospel of Thomas, were not inspired and so contain false words or nothing of significance.

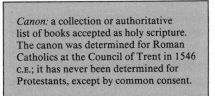

Canon: a collection or authoritative list of books accepted as holy scripture. The canon was determined for Roman Catholics at the Council of Trent in 1546 C.E.; it has never been determined for Protestants, except by common consent.

Scholars long ago abandoned this historically untenable and theologically naive view. Even conservative evangelical scholars concede that not every word ascribed to Jesus in the gospels was actually spoken by him. Scholars trained in the historical-critical method—the prevailing method in all historical disciplines—routinely distinguish sayings that originated with Jesus from those that were more likely created by the early Christian church or borrowed from common lore.

For more than two centuries scholars have studied the gospels using the tools of modern critical scholarship, the same tools employed in other humanistic and social scientific fields. They have reached certain broad conclusions, and like any historical science, the results of their investigations have been cumulative. But the public is poorly informed about those results. For this reason, a group of scholars formed the Jesus Seminar under the auspices of the Westar Institute to present their findings to the public. This is the first of a series of reports that presents those findings—findings that represent a consensus of current scholar-

1

ship. The first step in this report is to set out some of the obvious premises upon which any evaluation of the gospel materials must be based.

Aramaic and Greek

Jesus was a Galilean peasant who wrote nothing. His native tongue was Aramaic, whereas the records of what he said, created later by others, exist only in Greek, with a few texts in further translation preserved in Latin, or Coptic, or other ancient language. The tradition has preserved only a few Aramaic words attributed to Jesus.

Accordingly, if Jesus spoke only in Aramaic, his original words have been lost forever. The words of Jesus recorded in the gospels are thus at best a translation from Aramaic into Greek or some other ancient tongue.

Surviving Records

The original copies of written sources have completely disappeared. In fact, the oldest fragment of any portion of the New Testament now in existence dates from the second century C.E., one hundred years after Jesus' death. It is a tiny fragment of the Gospel of John. P⁵², as it is numbered in inventories of *papyri,* can be dated to about 125 C.E. (see reproduction pp. 44–45). A fragment of an unknown gospel, Papyrus Egerton 2, may be older than the John fragment; it is certainly older than all other surviving fragments or copies of canonical gospels. The next oldest fragments—of Matthew, Luke, John, Thomas—date to about 200 C.E. The first complete copy of the Greek New Testament known to us is the Codex Sinaiticus, discovered by Count Tischendorf in 1844 at the monastery of St. Catharine at the foot of Mount Sinai. It originated in the fourth century C.E. The "Catalogue of Select Greek Manuscripts" (pp. xvi) summarizes the early history of Greek manuscripts.

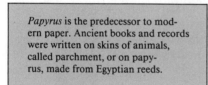

Papyrus is the predecessor to modern paper. Ancient books and records were written on skins of animals, called parchment, or on papyrus, made from Egyptian reeds.

In sum, three centuries separate Jesus from the earliest complete surviving copies of the gospels. One full century separates him from the earliest surviving fragment. Furthermore, no two copies or fragments are exactly alike, since they all predate the printing press.

There are about 5,000 Greek manuscripts that contain part or all of the New Testament. No two of them are exactly alike, since they were all copied by hand, and usually from dictation (one scribe read aloud, others copied). It was not until the invention of the printing press (1454 C.E.) that identical copies of the Bible could be readily reproduced on a large scale.

Before the Gospels

Written records of words attributed to Jesus undoubtedly go back well into the first century, perhaps even to a date as early as 50 C.E., a mere two decades after Jesus' death, although neither copies nor fragments from those early years have been discovered. However, before the gospels were written, and even after they were written, the lore about Jesus circulated primarily in oral form. Oral reminiscence rather than written record was the principal vehicle of transmission. The cultures and communities in which Christianity arose were essentially oral—all cultures were oral prior to the invention of writing, and most cultures, particularly those of the lower classes, continued to be oral until the invention of the printing press. In oral cultures and communities tradition is not fixed in writing, but is passed on as talk, and, as common experience proves, talk is more liquid, so to speak, than is writing. The fluidity of talk is restrained only by two factors. One is the structure of stories or sayings; the other is the use of fixed words or phrases. Otherwise, in oral communities purveyors of the tradition freely omitted, invented, modified, enlarged.

The different versions of the Golden Rule are a good example of the fluidity of oral tradition:

> And what you hate, do not do to any one.
> > *Tobit* 4:15
>
> And as you wish that men would do to you, do so to them.
> > Luke 6:31
>
> So whatever you wish that men would do to you, do so to them.
> > Matt 7:12
>
> Whatever you do not want done to you, do not do to another.
> > *Didache* 1:2

The precise wording varies from version to version. At the same time, all four are versions of the same wise saying or adage. Some are positive in form, others negative. Some of the same words occur, but the phrasing varies. The structure of the saying is constant. So it commonly is with oral tradition, even the tradition that preserves what Jesus said.

It may be possible to identify some of Jesus' words and the structure or outline of things he said, but it will never be possible to determine his exact words with absolute certainty since they were transmitted orally.

Tradition as Layers of Talk

Oral tradition is actually more complex than variations on a single strand of tradition, such as Jesus' words. It always consists of two or more layers of talk and these layers are so intertwined that it is difficult if not impossible to untangle them.

Scholars are fairly certain that Jesus talked a lot about the kingdom of God. In a sense, the gospels are records of Jesus talking about the kingdom of God. But they are more than that. They are also records of disciples talking about Jesus, who was himself talking about the kingdom of God. Talk about Jesus has already developed two layers or levels:

Level I   Jesus talking about: the kingdom of God
in parables
in short sayings or aphorisms

Level II   Disciples talking about: Jesus talking about the kingdom
in reminiscences of parables & sayings
in short stories of his actions

With the passing of the first generation of disciples, the Christian community, now the second generation, is still talking, orally, about Jesus. But now there are three layers: (3) the community is talking about (2) the disciples talking about (1) Jesus talking about the kingdom of God. And as the tradition matures, it becomes reflective about itself, as we all do as we age. A fourth layer of talk then emerges. (4) The community begins talking about (3) itself talking about (2) the disciples talking about (1)Jesus talking about the kingdom of God.

The question for scholars is how to distinguish these levels of talk, and especially, how to isolate Jesus' talk about the kingdom from other levels of talk in the written records, which is all we now have.

The oral transmission of the Jesus tradition did not end when the first written records appeared. Indeed, the primacy of oral transmission continued well into the second century. The living testimony of disciples and disciples of disciples remained more highly esteemed than the relatively rare and suspicious written text. Moreover, very few persons were wealthy enough to enjoy the possession and use of written copies of books. The Jesus tradition thus remained fluid for more than a century.

Jesus' saying about asking for a sign exhibits evidences of layering. The gospels record the saying in four different forms:

1. Why does this generation seek a sign? Truly, I say to you, no sign shall be given to this generation.   Mark 8:12

2a. *An evil and adulterous* generation seeks for a sign, but no sign shall be given to it *except the sign of Jonah.*   Matt 16:4

2b. This generation *is an evil generation; it* seeks a sign, but no sign shall be given to it *except the sign of Jonah.*   Luke 11:29

3. *An evil and adulterous* generation seeks for a sign, but no sign shall be given to it *except the sign of the prophet Jonah. For as Jonah was three nights in the belly of the whale, so will the Son of man be three days and three nights in the heart of the earth.*   Matt 12:39–40

Layers of Tradition

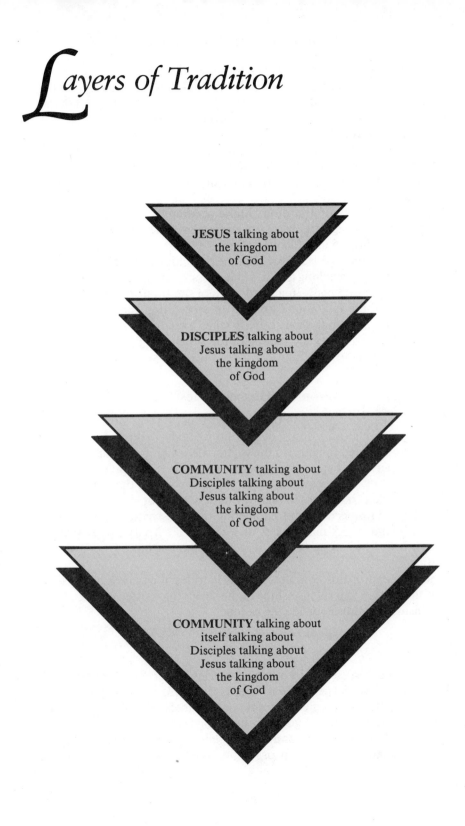

JESUS talking about
the kingdom
of God

DISCIPLES talking about
Jesus talking about
the kingdom
of God

COMMUNITY talking about
Disciples talking about
Jesus talking about
the kingdom
of God

COMMUNITY talking about
itself talking about
Disciples talking about
Jesus talking about
the kingdom
of God

Which of these sayings, if any, is original with Jesus?

According to Mark, Jesus states flatly that no sign shall be given to his generation. Matt 16:4 and Luke 11:29 qualify the saying with: "except the sign of Jonah." In this form, the sign of Jonah almost certainly refers to the preaching of Jonah.

But Matthew also preserves a more developed form in which the sign of Jonah is given a specifically Christian interpretation: the experience of Jonah in the belly of the whale prefigures the death, burial, and resurrection of Jesus.

On the first level of tradition, Mark accurately records Jesus' flat refusal to grant a sign (there is supporting evidence elsewhere in the tradition). In Matt 16 and Luke 11 there is a second level. The disciples have already qualified this refusal with the preaching of Jonah, since their work consisted of preaching and it was in response to preaching that they expected people to repent. In a third stage of the tradition, preserved in Matthew 12, there is a later Christian interpretation that represents a departure from anything Jesus said. It takes over Jonah's experience in the belly of the whale as the paradigm for Jesus and gives an elaborate theological account of the "sign."

From the Gospels to Jesus

We no longer have access to the oral tradition that was alive in the first hundred years or so after Jesus' death. But we do have immediate access, in Greek and related tongues, to the written deposit left by that tradition. We must therefore begin with the written records we have and work backwards. Working backwards requires that we search the written texts for clues of what transpired in their formation, of what took place during the oral period preceding and paralleling the first written gospels, and, finally, of what traces may be left of Jesus' own activity in our written sources. Jesus' own words lie, as it were, at the bottom of the layers of tradition.

The first step in this complex process is to learn as much as possible about the history and relationships of the surviving written gospels, both those inside and those outside the canon.

The Written Gospels

The written gospels fall into five categories, generally speaking. They are: (1) narrative gospels, (2) sayings gospels, (3) infancy gospels, (4) passion gospels, (5) fragments of unknown gospels and other fragments. The names attached to the gospels, including those included in the New Testament, are traditional, and in most cases do not provide any real information about authorship or origin. When the gospels emerge as written documents in history—when the first copies are made and circulated—author and place of origin have already been lost. The original composition of these gospels took place between 50 C.E. and the beginning of the third century C.E.

The Synoptic Gospels

The principal sources for the sayings of Jesus are the three Synoptic Gospels, Matthew, Mark, and Luke, together with the newly discovered Gospel of Thomas. The scholarly consensus on this point is almost universal.

Matthew, Mark, and Luke are often called Synoptic Gospels. Synoptic means that they share a common view of Jesus, as distinguished, for example, from the Gospel of John. When laid out in parallel columns in a gospel parallels or **synopsis,** the similarities between and among them are striking. One form of similarity is the extensive verbal agreement involving all three. The

> A *synopsis* arranges similar material side by side for comparison, whereas a harmony weaves the gospels into a single narrative strand. Critical scholars prefer synopses. *New Gospel Parallels* is a gospel synopsis incorporating the texts of all known written gospels.

Parable of the Mustard Seed illustrates a segment common to all three synoptic gospels. Another form of extensive verbal agreement links Matthew to Luke. In such instances, there is no parallel text in Mark. The parable of the Leaven is common to Matthew and Luke, but has no parallel in Mark. The remark-

> The German scholars who first proposed the *Q* hypothesis called the text on which Matthew and Luke drew "the source," which, in German, is *Quelle*. The designation is simply the initial letter of this word.

able verbal agreements in material common to these three gospels and in material common to Matthew and Luke only have led scholars for nearly two centuries to conclude that Matthew and Luke copied from Mark and from a second written source no longer directly available to us. This second source is known as **Q.** The striking verbal agreements must, of course, be observed in the original language, Greek.

A second type of similarity among the three Synoptics lies in the order of events and sayings. Matthew and Luke in general follow Mark's order when they are copying from him. By contrast, when Matthew and Luke are taking material from Q, they disperse the material in their gospels in very different ways.

To be sure, Matthew and Luke also have knowledge of still other traditions about Jesus which they incorporate into their gospels. For want of a better name, scholars refer to this material as special Matthew and special Luke. They do not necessarily represent written sources; the special material known to Matthew and Luke probably derives from oral tradition.

Mark & Q

A clear pattern emerges from the verbal agreements between and among the three synoptic evangelists.

• Matthew and Luke incorporate nearly all of Mark in their gospels. When copying Mark, Matthew and Luke generally follow his order of events and sayings.

• Mark contains very little material that Matthew and Luke have derived from Q and their special sources. Mark apparently does not know the other sources used by Matthew and Luke.

• Matthew and Luke incorporate large blocks of sayings material that are absent from Mark. Verbal agreement between Matthew and Luke is often high. This material does not appear in a common chronological order.

These complex relationships have prompted scholars to adopt the so-called four-source hypothesis: Matthew and Luke each utilize three sources. Matthew uses Mark, Q, and a special source; Luke uses Mark, Q, and a special source. The two special sources differ completely from each other. The four-source theory can be summarized graphically (see figure, p. 9). Put differently, Matthew and Luke used Mark as their first source (for the general outline), into which they have integrated materials from the Q-source. In addition, they incorporate materials available to them from two different special sources. No other explanation fits all the facts equally well.

Since both Matthew and Luke are dependent on the chronological outline of Mark, Mark is responsible for whatever chronology we have of the life of Jesus. Matthew and Luke have no independent knowledge of that chronology. This is supported by the fact that when they draw on Q, they do not agree about where items should be placed in the Markan outline.

The Q-source lacks chronology. Q is a collection of the sayings of Jesus arranged much like the Book of Proverbs. It contains very little biographical material; it has no birth or childhood stories and no passion narrative. It is a sayings gospel, much like the Gospel of Thomas. (See the "Catalogue of Written Gospels," pp. xvii–xx.)

Examples of Mark and Q Parables

The parable of the Sower (§19) appears in all three Synoptics. Matthew and Luke have thus copied and adapted it from Mark. The introduction, the parable itself, and the allegorical interpretation are shared by all three evangelists in quite similar language. The parable appears in the same relative order in all three gospels, except that Luke has moved the section on Jesus' true relatives from before to after the Sower.

The Four Source Theory

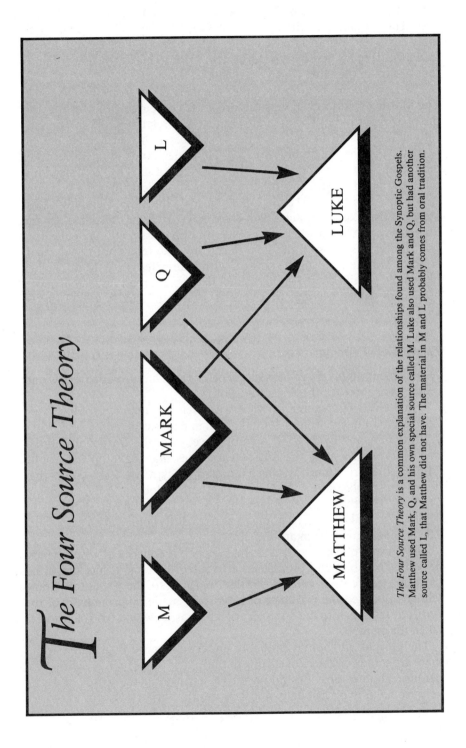

The Four Source Theory is a common explanation of the relationships found among the Synoptic Gospels. Matthew used Mark, Q, and his own special source called M. Luke also used Mark and Q, but had another source called L, that Matthew did not have. The material in M and L probably comes from oral tradition.

Similarly, the parable of the Tenants (§15) belongs to the triple tradition. The parable and the citation of scripture are quite similar in all
three texts and occur as part of the debate between Jesus and Jewish
leaders during his first days in Jerusalem prior to his death. The Tenants
thus occurs in the same relative position in the story.

The Lost Sheep (§8), on the other hand, is taken from the Q-source.
The Matthean and Lukan versions are quite comparable in wording, but
the placement in both immediate context and relative order is dramati-
cally different. Matthew situates the Lost Sheep in his sermon about who
is greatest in the kingdom (18:1–35). He understands the parable as an
indictment of those who despise the little ones. Luke, by contrast, combines the parable with two other parables about lost things: a lost coin
and a lost son (15:1–32). In Luke's gospel, the three parables—Lost
Sheep, Lost Coin, Prodigal Son—are part of Jesus' response to the
Pharisees and scribes when they object to him eating with tax-collectors
and sinners. As a result, the Lost Sheep in Luke refers not to the small
child of Matthew but to the sinners with whom Jesus ate. Matthew has
placed the parable in a sermon, while Luke locates it on Jesus' journey to
Jerusalem, which belongs to a special section of Luke's gospel (9:51–
19:27).

The Gospel of Thomas

The recent discovery of the Gospel of Thomas has provided a new and
important source for the Jesus tradition.

Three Greek fragments of what was then an unknown gospel were
discovered in Egypt around 1900 (known in papyrus inventories as POxy
1, POxy 654, and POxy 655). A complete copy of the Gospel of Thomas
was discovered among the fifty-two tractates that make up the Coptic
Gnostic Library found at Nag Hammadi, Egypt, in 1945. With that
discovery scholars knew the Greek fragments belonged to the Gospel of
Thomas. The three Greek fragments are all from different editions of
Thomas, so we know that Thomas was frequently copied at an early date.
The fragments date from around 200 C.E.

The Gospel of Thomas is a sayings gospel: it consists of wise sayings,
proverbs, parables and prophecies attributed to Jesus. It has almost no
narrative content; it is thus similar in form to the Q-source. Some
scholars doubted the existence of a "gospel" made up principally of the
words of Jesus before the discovery of Thomas; now that type of gospel is
taken for granted.

The Gospel of Thomas probably underwent more than one edition:
there are some evidences of editing in the text as we have it. Nevertheless,
because Thomas provides no narrative settings for the words of Jesus,
because he only occasionally appends interpretative words or allegories

to parables, and because his groupings of sayings are less developed, Thomas exhibits far less editorial activity, on the whole, than do the canonical gospels. Thomas also records items not found in other sources. Some but not all of these items have a **gnostic** tinge.

Thomas parallels the canonical gospels at numerous points. Most Fellows hold that Thomas is an independent witness to the Jesus tradition and is not dependent on the Synoptic Gospels (its closest rivals). There are four reasons for this:

> *Gnosticism* gets its name from the Greek word *gnosis* meaning knowledge or insight. For gnostics the world is divided into realms of darkness and light. The realm of darkness is the concrete world of sticks and stones, whereas the realm of light is above, completely segregated from the fallen world below. *Gnosis* is means of salvation for the selected few; it is means of finding one's way back to the heavens above. Gnostic gospels therefore gravitate to Jesus' instruction after his resurrection.

• There is no pattern of relationships between Thomas and the Synoptics that would require Thomas' dependence on them (contrast Matthew and Luke in relation to Mark).

• The order of items in Thomas is random in comparison with the Synoptics.

• The material in the Synoptics that is clearly the product of editorial activity is uniformly missing in Thomas; Thomas never reproduces the special theological perspectives of the Synoptics. This suggests that the tradition behind Thomas was reduced to writing before the Synoptic tradition achieved its final form.

• Thomas sometimes appears to be closer to an original version of a saying or parable.

Most Fellows of the Jesus Seminar agree that Thomas is an independent and valuable witness to the parables and sayings of Jesus.

The Gospel of John as a Source

The omission of the Gospel of John from the discussion of primary sources for the sayings of Jesus is striking and calls for explanation.

In the Synoptics and Thomas, Jesus speaks in **aphorisms** and in parables. In John, Jesus is represented as giving long, involved discourses, in which no parables appear and with only a rare aphorism embedded in an extended speech. In the first group of sources Jesus is a sage whose discourse is confined to proverbs, maxims, and parables, while in John Jesus is a philos-

> An *aphorism* is a short, pithy saying usually with a sharp edge. A proverb, or maxim, or adage, reflects common sense. A proverb: "the early bird catches the worm." An aphorism: "the first shall be last, and the last first."

opher, lecturer, and mystic. The difference in themes is also remarkable: in the Synoptics Jesus espouses the causes of the poor and downtrodden, the afflicted and the oppressed, but has relatively little to say about

11

himself; in John, by contrast, Jesus reflects extensively on his own mission and person and has little to say about the poor and oppressed.

Scholars generally agree that Jesus taught principally in aphorisms and parables; they therefore hold that the picture drawn of him in the Synoptics and Thomas is more accurate than the one painted by the Fourth Evangelist. The Gospel of John, consequently, is not a reliable source for what Jesus said, although it may provide other valuable information.

Date and Authorship of Written Gospels

The earliest written sources for the Jesus tradition are Q and Thomas in its original form. Scholars speculate that the original versions of Q and Thomas were composed around 50–60 C.E., a scant two or three decades after Jesus' death. Both documents went through revisions, perhaps more than once, in which new material was added and old material modified. The second editions of each also predate the canonical gospels and probably the fall of Jerusalem (70 C.E.). The authors are unknown.

An anonymous author composed the Gospel of Mark shortly after the destruction of Jerusalem, as Mark 13 implies. Matthew and Luke made use of Mark barely a decade later in creating their own gospels, so Mark became established quickly.

Mark is responsible for forming the first chronological outline of the life of Jesus. He may also be responsible for the first connected account of Jesus' passion (Mark 14–16). Mark reports more deeds than words of Jesus in comparison with Q and Thomas, Matthew and Luke. He reflects the conviction of the Christian community that God was about to bring the world to an end in an apocalyptic conflagration.

Someone compiled the Gospel of Matthew after the fall of Jerusalem (70 C.E.), during the period when the Christian community was seeking its own identity over against Judaism, and when Judaism was attempting to recover from the loss of the center of its worship, the temple. Matthew mirrors the pain suffered by Christians when they were excluded from the synagogue (Matt 5:10–13). This period of adjustment for both Christianity and Judaism took place between 70 C.E. and the Council of Jamnia in 90 C.E., when rabbinic Judaism took shape. Matthew can therefore be dated to about 85 C.E., give or take a few of years.

Luke–Acts, a two volume work by a single author, depicts the emergence of Christianity on the world stage. It belongs to the same period as Matthew. Whereas Matthew was concerned with the Jewish reaction to Christianity, Luke is preoccupied with developments among the Gentiles. The first volume begins with a formal dedication to a Greek nobleman, Theophilus, and the second concludes with Paul preaching in the first city of the Mediterranean world, Rome.

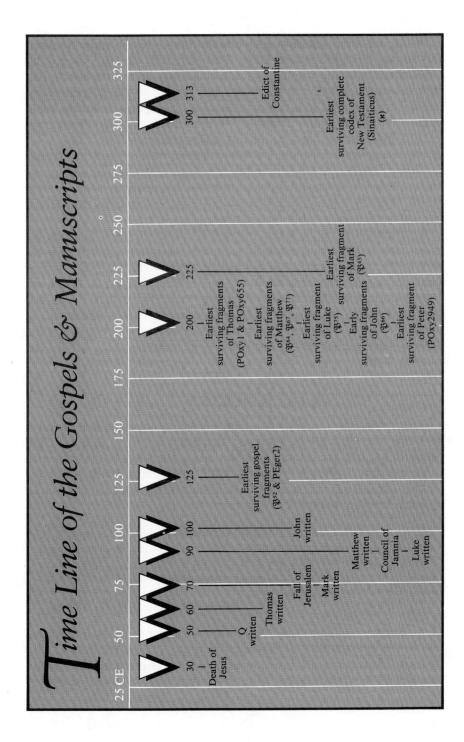

Time Line of the Gospels & Manuscripts

25 CE   50   75   100   125   150   175   200   225   250   275   300   325

30 — Death of Jesus

50 — Q written

60 — Thomas written

70 — Fall of Jerusalem
Mark written

90 — Matthew written
Council of Jamnia
Luke written

100 — John written

125 — Earliest surviving gospel fragments ($\mathfrak{P}^{52}$ & PEger2)

200 — Earliest surviving fragments of Thomas (POxy 1 & POxy655)
Earliest surviving fragments of Matthew ($\mathfrak{P}^{64}$, $\mathfrak{P}^{67}$, $\mathfrak{P}^{77}$)
Earliest surviving fragment of Luke ($\mathfrak{P}^{75}$)
Early surviving fragments of John ($\mathfrak{P}^{66}$)
Earliest surviving fragment of Peter (POxy2949)

225 — Earliest surviving fragment of Mark ($\mathfrak{P}^{45}$)

300 — Earliest surviving complete codex of New Testament (Sinaiticus) ($\aleph$)

313 — Edict of Constantine

Assessment of Written Sources

The nature of the written gospels and the literary relationships between and among them prompt scholars to be extremely cautious in making judgments about the originality of specific bits of the tradition. The chronological arrangement of events and sayings in the gospels is extremely arbitrary and so is not reliable. Mark is responsible for the basic outline. However, Q and Thomas, Matthew and Luke, also create contexts for given items that are probably no less arbitrary.

The evangelists arranged materials with great freedom and interpreted the same materials in quite different ways. They were not simply conserving or reporting the traditions about Jesus, but adapting them to new needs. These factors alone make scholars wary of recovering the specific original wording of parables and sayings.

Variations in the polls taken among Fellows of the Jesus Seminar on given items indicate that scholarly judgments are rarely uniform. Nevertheless, the trend of critical assessment is abundantly clear: only a very small portion of the words attributed to Jesus actually go back to him. The proportion of authentic parables is perhaps higher than is the case with short sayings (to be reported in a subsequent volume). The parables, it seems, were more difficult to imitate because less widely used in the ancient world and because Jesus achieved a consummate artistry in creating them.

Parables: the Bedrock of the Tradition

Joachim Jeremias, one of the great parable scholars of this century, held that the parables of Jesus are the bedrock of the tradition. He believed that with the genuine parables one is very close to the authentic voice of Jesus (*The Parables of Jesus*, 11). Like Jeremias, Norman Perrin, another parable scholar, was convinced that the parables are distinctive of Jesus. They are so distinctive, in fact,

> that in broad structural outline they survived the subsequent process of transmission very well, while, at the same time, the process of reinterpretation was so obvious and so much at variance with the original thrust of the parables themselves, that the original form and thrust of the parables have not proven difficult to reconstruct.
>
> —*Jesus and the Language of the Kingdom*, 3

These comments identify the two categories that have played a central role in the deliberations of the Jesus Seminar: (1) the parables as distinctive instruments of Jesus' speech; (2) the reinterpretation of the parables as they were taken up into the tradition and used in altered

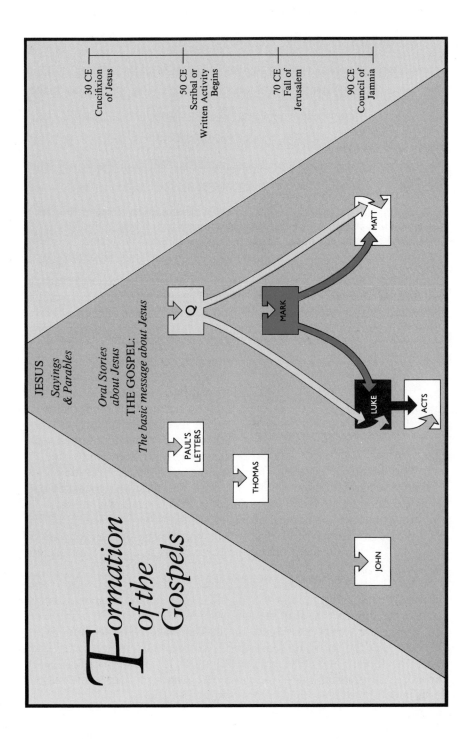

_F_ormation
of the
Gospels

JESUS
Sayings
& Parables

Oral Stories
about Jesus

THE GOSPEL:
The basic message about Jesus

PAUL'S
LETTERS

THOMAS

Q

MARK

MATT

LUKE

ACTS

JOHN

30 CE
Crucifixion
of Jesus

50 CE
Scribal or
Written Activity
Begins

70 CE
Fall of
Jerusalem

90 CE
Council of
Jamnia

situations to meet new problems. Scholars attempt to distinguish the first from the second.

The parables as distinctive creations of Jesus bear certain distinguishing marks. The written records sometimes offer clues that enable us to discriminate what stems from Jesus from what is secondary. These marks and clues are either strong or weak criteria. The strong criteria are listed first.

Marks of the Genuine Parables of Jesus

C. H. Dodd, the British counterpart to the German Jeremias, has provided a classic definition of the parable.

> At its simplest the parable is a metaphor or simile drawn from nature or common life, arresting the hearer by its vividness or strangeness, and leaving the mind in sufficient doubt about its precise application to tease it into active thought.   *—The Parables of the Kingdom,* 16

From this definition derive four essential clues to the parables of Jesus.

1. The parable is a **metaphor** or **simile.** The metaphor may be simple, elaborated as a picture, or expanded into a story. If Jesus talks constantly about the kingdom of God, he is comparing the kingdom with a mustard seed or a quest for a lost coin, or a mugging on the Jericho road. He does not specify how the two are to be compared. He simply sets them side by side and lets them resonate for the listener. Resonate is the correct word, because his comparisons customarily jar, stand in tension.

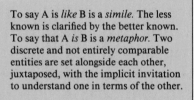

To say A is *like* B is a *simile.* The less known is clarified by the better known. To say that A *is* B is a *metaphor.* Two discrete and not entirely comparable entities are set alongside each other, juxtaposed, with the implicit invitation to understand one in terms of the other.

2. The metaphor is taken from nature or common, everyday life. Initially, the parable draws on a picture or situation that is typical of what everyone knows and takes for granted: a master calling a steward to account, a banquet, the harvest of grapes, a buried treasure. The situation need not be precisely typical: it may only represent what everyone takes as typical. So children are prodigal, stewards cheat, and every Californian would like to win the lottery.

3. Yet the metaphor taken from nature or the everyday world, the received world, arrests the hearer by its vividness or strangeness. Jesus chooses metaphors that surprise (the leaven as a figure for the holy), or that exaggerate (everyone refuses the invitation to come to dinner), or that satirize (the mustard plant pokes fun at the mighty cedar that represents Israel). The reader must always look for the surprising twist in the story, the unusual figure, the paradoxical pattern. This is the reason Jesus' metaphors create tension or resonate (see clue 1).

4. The parable has no conclusion. It always teases the hearer with its possible application. Since the parables were probably told in a variety of situations by Jesus, we cannot always be sure of how he used them. But we can *imagine* situations to which they may have been applied or into which they may have been spoken. That imagination must be disciplined, however, by historical knowledge of Jesus' time and place. Jesus himself never explicitly tells us how he meant them to be understood.

In addition to these four distinctive features of Jesus' parables, one other strong characteristic may be noted:

5. The genuine parables of Jesus are narratives and thus will also exhibit a characteristic plot structure. A common plot involves the reversal of roles. The participant who expects to succeed or be rewarded is disappointed, whereas the one who has no right to fare well or receive a prize is surprised. "He who is last shall be first, and the first last" is a characteristic aphorism of Jesus as well as a characteristic plot of his parables. The genuine parables also manifest other plot structures.

Three other clues, relatively weak on the scale of criteria, are also invoked in scholarly evaluations.

6. Genuine parables of Jesus will exhibit the marks of oral composition.

• A tight, lean, compressed style. No more words than necessary (the parsimony of language). Example: the Leaven (§1).

• Uncomplicated plots and the use of pairs and sets of three. The good guys and bad guys are clearly identified; the principal players are often two in number; things happen in sets of three. Example: the Good Samaritan (§2).

• Concrete, vivid images. Abstractions are more characteristic of written composition than oral creation. Allegory fits writing better than speaking. Example of abstraction: the allegorical interpretation of the Sower (§19) and the Planted Weeds (§25). Examples of concrete vivid images: the Vineyard Laborers (§4) and the Lost Coin (§6).

7. The sources in which parables are found offer weak critera. Theoretically, genuine parables will be found in sources that are more likely to preserve oral tradition. Unfortunately, this clue is not much help in practice, since all five basic sources—Mark, Q, Thomas, Special Matthew, Special Luke—can and do record items close to the oral tradition. The basis for evaluation is firmer if a parable or saying is reported in two or more independent sources, such as Q and Thomas, or Thomas and the Synoptics (parables are listed by source on p. 82). The close comparison of independent versions greatly assists in the identification of intrusive elements.

8. One final weak clue concerns the written context in which a parable appears. If the parable itself is at odds with the context in which the evangelist places the parable, we have weak evidence that the parable

predates the work of the evangelist. This is essentially a negative clue, but it often plays a significant role in textual analysis.

9. These features and clues are not always obvious. In evaluations, arguments and disputes abound. Some parables are simply marginal cases. When in doubt, scholars put the parable under review to the final test of a reading: can one read or interpret this parable in a way that coheres with other authentic (or inauthentic) parables in the tradition?

For example, if the parable of the Good Samaritan (§2) is an example story that illustrates what it is like to be a good neighbor, it is probably not a parable of Jesus. But if it is a metaphor that hints at what it is like to receive help from an alien, from an enemy, then it is metaphorical and may be a genuine parable. The modern reading of the Samaritan has convinced many scholars that it is a genuine parable.

The Empty Jar (§21) in the Gospel of Thomas is viewed with suspicion by many scholars because they cannot imagine a situation in which Jesus might have used it. On the other hand, the jar with the hole in it causes the woman to loose all her meal on the way home. That strikes some interpreters as an everyday but surprising image. It reverses the expected image of the full jar as the proper metaphor for the kingdom: the woman arrives home, not with an abundance of meal, but with an empty jar. It also exhibits Jesus' use of ordinary tasks and implements in his stories. The final evaluation of this parable turns on how it is interpreted.

Clues to Secondary Layers

The written gospels also provide clues to secondary additions, omissions, inventions, modifications. These clues are again strong or weak. They are ordered once more from the stronger to the weaker.

1. Interpretative changes take one of four forms:

(a) Secondary context: scholars always assume that the context in which the evangelist places a given parable is secondary. Parables were probably circulated orally without context, the context being provided by the occasion on which the parable was spoken. The evangelists, or a source before them, have invented contexts for the parables.

(b) Interpretative conclusions: there is a tendency to add interpretative conclusions to parables, sometimes more than one. Such conclusions often take the form of aphorisms. Interpretative conclusions are always secondary, although the aphorism so appended may itself be authentic. (See clue 4 above)

(c) Frequently the body of a parable will have been modified to make it conform to the literary context in which it has been placed or to serve the special interests of a particular evangelist. Such modifications may be modest or massive.

(d) Parables may be linked with other parables or other materials in order to "place" them. For example, the Leaven and the Mustard Seed were linked early in the tradition, although they did not originally belong together. As a result of the linking, they came to be interpreted in a similar way. Linking is of course a subtle form of contextualizing.

All of these forms of modification require the scholar to be constantly on guard against the special interests of particular evangelists. Naturally, where those interests have prompted one or the other form of modification, the scholar seeks to go behind that modification to a layer that can be understood as more typical of Jesus.

2. A second clue to secondary layering is evidence of the subsequent social situation of the Christian community.

Jesus was an itinerant sage. He apparently belonged to no established community. He seems to have broken social barriers right and left and advocated that others do so. He favored including the poor and oppressed, the religiously and socially disinherited. On the other hand, the early community soon became a church, an established community, with its own lines of social demarcation. Those lines included discriminating those who adhered to the community rules from those who did not. Consequently, scholars are on the lookout for traces of a secondary social context.

3. A third clue involves borrowing from common wisdom.

Jesus is reported to have said, "Those who are well have no need of a doctor, only those who are sick" (Mark 2:17). It is quite possible that he did. However, that same adage is attested, in one form or another, in many ancient sources, some of which predate Jesus, and it is attributed to more than one sage. The question then becomes: Did Jesus really say that, or did his reputation as a sage prompt the early community to attribute common wisdom to him?

On balance, scholars are inclined to think that Jesus attracted attributions of well-known sayings and parables, rather than that he borrowed freely from common lore. He may, of course, have said some or many commonplace things. If so, such sayings are no help in distinguishing Jesus from the ordinary sage. Scholars are thus hesitant to employ common wisdom in the written sources as a strong clue to Jesus' identity.

The Jesus Seminar: Procedures

The Jesus Seminar adopted specific goals and procedures.

The goal was to evaluate all the parables and sayings attributed to Jesus in the first three centuries and arrange them on a scale from those Jesus almost certainly said to those he almost certainly did not say. The ranking was to be determined by scholarly consensus.

The first step was to create the inventory by classifying all the words attributed to Jesus by both form and source. The parables were identified and entered into the inventory by source, with versions of the same parable grouped together for easy comparison. The second category consisted of aphorisms, the third of dialogues, and the fourth of stories with words of Jesus embedded. The result was *Sayings Parallels* containing over a thousand versions of 503 items.

Because the parables have long been considered the bedrock of the Jesus tradition, the Seminar decided to start with the thirty-three parables in the inventory. Next on the agenda are the aphorisms of Jesus, to be followed by the stories and dialogues containing words attributed to Jesus.

The Jesus Seminar meets twice yearly, in the spring and in the fall. The Steering Committee establishes an agenda for each meeting. Prior to the meeting, a preliminary poll on the items scheduled to be discussed is taken. The results are used to allot discussion time: those items on which a strong consensus already exists are not discussed; the Seminar devotes its time to items on which opinion is divided.

Scholarly papers are prepared on each item in advance of meetings. The papers are duplicated and circulated to Fellows and Associates for advance review. The meetings themselves are devoted to discussion and debate.

At the conclusion of each meeting, a second and presumably final poll is taken. The results are reported in *The Forum*, a journal designed for members of the Westar Institute, a research institute located in Sonoma, California. Occasionally, the results are not conclusive, so items are reconsidered at subsequent meetings. Upon occasion, additional studies are prepared by individual scholars and circulated to the group. Any member may call for reconsideration of any item.

The method of polling has attracted wide attention.

Using traditional red letter editions of the New Testament as the model, the Fellows decided to make red and black the basic categories: words that approximate the voice of Jesus were to be designated red, in accordance with the red letter tradition. Words not representative of him were to be left in black. The group then determined that it needed at least two intermediate categories. One, pink, was a weak form of red, while gray was to be understood as a step up from black. The four colors thus represent a scale of 0 to 3, with red at the upper end, and black at the lower end. The Seminar employed colored beads dropped into voting boxes in order to permit scholars to vote in secret.

The Seminar adopted two official interpretations of the four colors (see the box). Individuals could adopt either one, or understand the colors in some other way. The Seminar did not insist on uniform standards for balloting.

Option 1

Red: I would include this item unequivocally in the data base for determining who Jesus was.

Pink: I would include this item with reservations (or modifications) in the data base for determining who Jesus was.

Gray: I would not include this item in the primary data base, but I might make use of some of the content in determining who Jesus was.

Black: I would not include this item in the primary data base for determining who Jesus was.

Option 2

Red: Jesus undoubtedly said this or something very like it.

Pink: Jesus probably said something like this.

Gray: Jesus did not say this, but the ideas contained in it are close to his own.

Black: Jesus did not say this; it represents the perspective or content of a later or different tradition.

The classification of parables and sayings is determined by weighted vote. Red votes receive 3 points, pink votes 2 points, gray votes 1 points, and black votes 0. The points on each ballot are added up and divided by the number of voters in order to determine the weighted average. A parable receiving a weighted average of 0.75 or under is black; 0.751–1.50 is the gray spectrum; 1.501–2.25 is the pink; and 2.251 and above is red. These ranges divide the weighted averages into four equal groups corresponding to the four colors.

This system, which greatly simplifies the procedures, replaces an older one, reported in the *Forum*, according to which a parable had to receive a 2/3 majority of red/pink to be included in the authentic data base, or a 2/3 majority of gray/black to be excluded. The earlier system left the Seminar with a several unresolved problems.

For reasons already advanced, some Fellows were unable to vote red on any item. They might hold, for example, that Jesus' original words were Aramaic so we have nothing that goes back literally to him. Or, their view may be that oral tradition never preserves words literally, only the general sense. For a few Fellows the highest category was gray. So far as is known, every Fellow was willing to vote black on a given item. Several votes on interpretative conclusions appended to parables were voted black by acclamation (common consent). As a consequence, the vote tends to be skewed towards the black end of the spectrum.

The results are reported in the red letter edition of the parables that forms the substance of this volume.

How to Use This Book

The results of the deliberations of the Fellows of the Jesus Seminar are reported by color code in the "Texts and Notes" to follow.

The parables are printed in the order of their weighted votes, those with the highest weighted averages coming first. Exceptions to this rule: where more than one version of a parable is involved, the version with the highest weighted average determines the relative position of that parable in the listing. All other versions of the same parable are printed on the same page or two-page spread to facilitate comparison.

Two versions of the Leaven, for example, are printed in red and have the highest weighted averages of all parables (Table 7, pp. 104–5). The Leaven therefore comes first in the listing. Although the Thomas version is pink, it nevertheless accompanies the Matthean and Lukan versions of the Leaven.

The thirty-three parables are thus grouped according to the color of the version with the highest weighted average. The red parables (five) come first, followed by the pink (16); gray (six) comes next, and then black (six). Table 1 (pp. 26–27) is a guide to this grouping.

If separate votes were taken on parts of parables, these votes are reported separately both in the color coding and by bar graph.

Bar graphs accompany the presentation of each parable and version. The bars represent the weighted vote on each version. Table 7 (pp. 104–5) gives the absolute ranking of all sixty versions of thirty three parables. Table 7 is thus a summary of the information provided by the bar graphs.

Notes accompany each parable. The notes are intended to provide a brief account of the reasons advanced by Fellows for ranking the parable or version as they did.

The written source for each parable or version is also indicated on each page or spread. The list of "Parables by Source" (p. 82) summarizes this information.

Additional statistical tables appear as appendices. Table 4 ranks parables by the percentage of red vote, Table 5 by percentage of black vote. Table 6 combines percentages of the red/pink vote and the gray/black. Parables are ranked by percentage of red/pink vote in descending order and by percentage of gray/black vote in ascending order. As indicated above, Table 7 provides the absolute ranking of all versions and Table 8 lists parts of parables by weighted vote.

For the convenience of readers, Tables 2 and 3 afford a summary of parables deemed authentic (receiving a weighted average of 1.501 or higher) and those deemed inauthentic (parables receiving a weighted average of 1.50 or less).

The names and institutions of the Fellows of the Seminar form another appendix. Some Fellows elected not to have their names included in this list for one reason or another. The directory of Fellows is accompanied by a brief essay on the standards of critical scholarship.

Also included in the appendices is a sketch of the recent history of parable interpretation, which amounts to a brief catalogue of modern parable scholars. Another appendix offers reading suggestions for those who wish to pursue the study of parables.

The reader needs to exercise caution in interpreting the results. The Fellows represent a wide range of methodologies, presuppositions, and perspectives. The polls thus indicate a scholarly consensus only in a broad sense. In spite of the divergence in methodology and perspective, the results are nevertheless indicative of broad trends. In general the conclusions to which Fellows came were to be expected: there are very few undisputed red and black parables, relatively more pink and gray, because it is difficult to achieve certainty where oral tradition and tardy written sources provide the basic data.

The Seminar elected to make its report to the public in the form of a critical red letter edition of the parables because only in that form would it be accessible to a broad public and at a glance. This red letter edition, which is based on literary and historical evidence, stands in stark contrast, moreover, to the traditional uncritical red letter editions based on authoritarian theological dogmas or claims. This edition permits the reader to see the constructive possibilities for understanding how Christianity developed under the conditions of an oral culture centuries before the invention of the printing press.

*W*hat Is A Critical
Red Letter Edition?

In the traditional red letter Bible, all the words ascribed to Jesus in the whole of the New Testament are printed in red. Jesus is not only made to say, "If any one strikes you on the right cheek, turn to him the other also" (Matt 5:39), he is also represented as saying, "Behold, I will throw her [the woman Jezebel] on a sickbed, and those who commit adultery with her I will throw into great tribulation, unless they repent of her doings; and I will strike her children dead" (Rev 2:22–23). The stark contrast in content makes one wonder whether the same Jesus is speaking.

In some red letter versions, the words ascribed to Jesus in the Book of Revelation are not printed in red. Ecclesiastical officials, who generally control these decisions, are understandably hesitant to identify the blood-thirsty figure of Revelation with the peacemaker of the gospels. They probably also want to distinguish words spoken by Jesus in public from those spoken by a heavenly figure privately, usually in dreams or visions, and reported by third parties. And they may be concerned to segregate the words of the earthly Jesus from those allegedly spoken by an ethereal Jesus. In other words, they are attempting to circumscribe what may be credited as words spoken by Jesus of Nazareth.

Unless limits are placed on the process, there would be no end in principle to what may be reported as words of Jesus. In the first days of the Jesus Seminar, an individual in Los Angeles submitted a thick document to the Seminar for critical review. The document contained thousands of words revealed directly to that person, allegedly by Jesus. Fortunately, the Seminar had already decided to limit its review and evaluation to words reported in written documents in the first three centuries C.E.

In distinguishing words ascribed to Jesus in the four gospels from words attributed to Jesus in the Book of Revelation, the editors of some traditional red letter editions are producing a "critical" edition. A critical edition is nothing more or less than an edition in which certain discriminations are made.

The Parables of Jesus: Red Letter Edition is a critical edition in which parables that originated with Jesus are distinguished from parables that came into the tradition from common lore or were created by the Christian community.

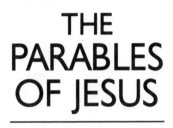

THE
PARABLES
OF JESUS

Table of Parables

Red Parables

1. *Leaven*
   - Matt 13:33b
   - Luke 13:20b–21
   - Thom 96:1
2. *Good Samaritan*
   - Luke 10:30b–35
   - Luke 10:36–37
3. *Dishonest Steward*
   - Luke 16:1–8a
   - Luke 16:8b–9
4. *Vineyard Laborers*
   - Matt 20:1–15
5. *Mustard Seed*
   - Matt 13:31b–32
   - Mark 4:31–32
   - Luke 13:19
   - Thom 20:2

Pink Parables

6. *Lost Coin*
   - Luke 15:8–9
   - Luke 15:10
7. *Treasure*
   - Matt 13:44
   - Thom 109
8. *Lost Sheep*
   - Matt 18:12–13
   - Matt 18:14
   - Luke 15:4–6
   - Luke 15:7
   - Thom 107
9. *Prodigal Son*
   - Luke 15:11b–32
10. *Unjust Judge*
    - Luke 18:2–5
    - Luke 18:6b–8
11. *Feast*
    - Matt 22:2–13
    - Luke 14:16b–23
    - Luke 14:24
    - Thom 64:1
    - Thom 64:2
12. *Pearl*
    - Matt 13:45–46
    - Thom 76:1
13. *Seed and Harvest*
    - Mark 4:26b–29
    - Thom 21:4
14. *Unmerciful Servant*
    - Matt 18:23–34
    - Matt 18:35
15. *Tenants*
    - Matt 21:33b–39
    - Matt 21:40–43
    - Mark 12:1b–8
    - Mark 12:9–11
    - Luke 20:9b–15a
    - Luke 20:15b–18
    - Thom 65
    - Thom 66
16. *Rich Farmer*
    - Luke 12:16b–20
    - Luke 12:21
    - Thom 63:1
17. *Entrusted Money*
    - Matt 25:14–21b, 22–23b, 24–28
    - Matt 25:21c, 23c, 29–30
    - Luke 19:13, 15–24
    - Luke 19:12, 14, 25–27
    - GNaz 18
18. *Pharisee and Publican*
    - Luke 18:10–14a
19. *Sower*
    - Matt 13:3b–8
    - Matt 13:18–23
    - Mark 4:3b–8
    - Mark 4:14–20
    - Luke 8:5–8a
    - Luke 8:11–15
    - Thom 9
    - 1 Clement 24:5
20. *Barren Tree*
    - Luke 13:6b–9
21. *Empty Jar*
    - Thom 97

Table 1

Gray Parables

22. *Returning Master*
    - Mark 13:34–36
    - Mark 13:37
    - Luke 12:35–38
    - Didache 16:1a
23. *Assassin*
    - Thom 98
24. *Rich Man and Lazarus*
    - Luke 16:19–26
    - Luke 16:27–31
25. *Planted Weeds*
    - Matt 13:24b–30
    - Matt 13:37–43a
    - Thom 57
26. *Ear of Grain*
    - ApJas 8:2b
27. *Closed Door*
    - Matt 25:1–12
    - Matt 25:13
    - Luke 13:25

Black Parables

28. *Tower Builder*
    - Luke 14:28–30
29. *Warring King*
    - Luke 14:31–32
    - Luke 14:33
30. *Fishnet*
    - Matt 13:47–48
    - Matt 13:49–50
    - Thom 8:1
31. *Grain of Wheat*
    - ApJas 6:11b
32. *Palm Shoot*
    - ApJas 6:8b
33. *Children in the Field*
    - Thom 21:1–2

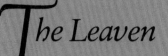he Leaven

in Greek & Coptic

MATT

Matthew 13:33 in Greek
³³ Ἄλλην παραβολὴν
ἐλάλησεν αὐτοῖς· Ὁμοία
ἐστὶν ἡ βασιλεία τῶν
οὐρανῶν ζύμῃ, ἣν λαβοῦσα
γυνὴ ἐνέκρυψεν εἰς ἀλεύρου
σάτα τρία ἕως οὗ ἐζυμώθη
ὅλον.

LUKE

Luke 13:20–21 in Greek
²⁰ Καὶ πάλιν εἶπεν· Τίνι
ὁμοιώσω τὴν βασιλείαν τοῦ
θεοῦ; ²¹ ὁμοία ἐστὶν ζύμῃ, ἣν
λαβοῦσα γυνὴ [ἐν]έκρυψεν
εἰς ἀλεύρου σάτα τρία ἕως οὗ
ἐζυμώθη ὅλον.

THOM

Thomas 96 in Coptic
[ⲡⲉϫⲉ] ⲓ̅ⲥ̅ ϫⲉ ⲧⲙⲛⲧⲉⲣⲟ
ⲙ̅ⲡⲉⲓⲱⲧ ⲉⲥⲧⲛ̅ⲧⲱ[ⲛ
ⲉⲟⲩ]ⲥϩⲓⲙⲉ ⲁⲥϫⲓ
ⲛ̅ⲟⲩⲕⲟⲅⲉⲓ ⲛ̅ⲥⲁⲉⲓⲣ[(ⲉ)
ⲁⲥϩⲟ]ⲡϥ ϩⲛ̅ ⲟⲩϣⲱⲧⲉ
ⲁⲥⲁⲁϥ ⲛ̅ϩⲛ̅ⲛⲟ[ϭ] ⲛ̅ⲟⲉⲓⲕ
ⲡⲉⲧⲉⲩⲙ̅ ⲙⲁⲁϫⲉ ⲙ̅ⲙⲟϥ
ⲙⲁ[ⲣⲉϥ]ⲥⲱⲧⲙ.

 *eaven*

Matthew 13:33b
³³ He told them another parable. "The kingdom of heaven is like leaven which a woman took and hid in three measures of flour, till it was all leavened."

Luke 13:20b–21
²⁰ And again he said, "To what shall I compare the kingdom of God? ²¹ It is like leaven which a woman took and hid in three measures of flour, till it was all leavened."

Thomas 96:1
¹ Jesus [said], "The Kingdom of the Father is like a certain woman. She took a little leaven, [concealed] it in some dough, and made it into large loaves.
² Let him who has ears hear."

Exodus 12:15: "Seven days you shall eat unleavened bread; on the first day you shall put away leaven out of your houses, for if any one eats what is leavened, . . . that person shall be cut off from Israel."
Mark 8:15: "And he cautioned them, saying, 'Take heed, beware of the leaven of the Pharisees and the leaven of Herod.'"
1 Corinthians 5:7: "Cleanse out the old leaven that you may be fresh dough, as you really are unleavened."

Matt 13:33b
Luke 13:20b–21
Thom 96:1

Sources: *Q and Thomas*

Notes

The parable of the Leaven transmits the voice of Jesus as clearly as any ancient written record can, in the judgment of most Fellows of the Jesus Seminar.

The Matthean and Lukan versions were considered more original than the version in Thomas because the contrast of "little leaven—large loaves" has been introduced into the parable by Thomas. This contrast, found also in the parables of the Lost Sheep (§8) and the Fishnet (§30), is alien to the genuine parables of Jesus.

Jesus employs the image of the leaven in a highly provocative way. In Passover observance, Judaism regarded leaven as a symbol of corruption, while unleaven stood for what was holy.

The Leaven provides a surprising reversal of expectations—leaven representing the kingdom of God—a strategy Fellows believe to be typical of Jesus.

The parable of the Leaven exhibits marks of oral tradition: it is short and tightly composed and has no superfluous words. In addition, the nearly exact verbal agreement of Matthew and Luke indicates that neither edited the parable.

Matthew's preference for the kingdom of heaven and Luke's use of the kingdom of God is a matter of style. Normal Jewish usage avoided the name of God, for which heaven was substituted. As a gospel especially concerned with relations to Judaism, Matthew maintains this usage.

Thom 96:2 is an independent saying frequently added to parables and other sayings attributed to Jesus. The Jesus Seminar will consider this aphorism separately.

Good Samaritan

Matt 22:34–40

³⁴ But when the Pharisees heard that he had silenced the Sadducees, they came together. ³⁵ And one of them, a lawyer, asked him a question, to test him. ³⁶ "Teacher, which is the great commandment in the law?" ³⁷ And he said to him, "You shall love the Lord your God with all your heart, and with all your soul, and with all your mind. ³⁸ This is the great and first commandment. ³⁹ And a second is like it, You shall love your neighbor as yourself. ⁴⁰ On these two commandments depend all the law and the prophets."

Mark 12:28–34

²⁸ And one of the scribes came up and heard them disputing with one another, and seeing that he answered them well, asked him, "Which commandment is the first of all?" ²⁹ Jesus answered, "The first is, 'Hear, O Israel: The Lord our God, the Lord is one; ³⁰ and you shall love the Lord your God with all your heart, and with all your soul, and with all your mind, and with all your strength.' ³¹ The second is this, 'You shall love your neighbor as yourself.' There is no other commandment greater than these." ³² And the scribe said to him, "You are right, Teacher; you have truly said that he is one, and there is no other but he; ³³ and to love him with all the heart, and with all the understanding, and with all the strength, and to love one's neighbor as oneself, is much more than all whole burnt offerings and sacrifices." ³⁴ And when Jesus saw that he answered wisely, he said to him, "You are not far from the kingdom of God." And after that no one dared to ask him any question.

Luke 10:30–37

²⁵ And behold, a lawyer stood up to put him to the test, saying, "Teacher, what shall I do to inherit eternal life?" ²⁶ He said to him, "What is written in the law? How do you read?" ²⁷ And he answered, "You shall love the Lord your God with all your heart, and with all your soul, and with all your strength, and with all your mind; and your neighbor as yourself." ²⁸ And he said to him, "You have answered right; do this, and you will live."

²⁹ But he, desiring to justify himself, said to Jesus, "And who is my neighbor?" ³⁰ Jesus replied, "A man was going down from Jerusalem to Jericho, and he fell among robbers, who stripped him and beat him, and departed, leaving him half dead. ³¹ Now by chance a priest was going down that road; and when he saw him he passed by on the other side. ³² So likewise a Levite, when he came to the place and saw him, passed by on the other side. ³³ But a Samaritan, as he journeyed, came to where he was; and when he saw him, he had compassion, ³⁴ and went to him and bound up his wounds, pouring on oil and wine; then he set him on his own beast and brought him to an inn, and took care of him. ³⁵ And the next day he took out two denarii and gave them to the innkeeper, saying, 'Take care of him; and whatever more you spend, I will repay you when I come back.'

³⁶ **"Which of these three, do you think, proved neighbor to the man who fell among the robbers?" ³⁷ He said, "The one who showed mercy on him." And Jesus said to him, "Go and do likewise."**

Luke 10:30b–35
Luke 10:36–37

30

The modern road between Jerusalem and Jericho runs past the Khan Hathrur, a caravansary, traditionally identified as the inn of the Good Samaritan.

Source: *Luke*

Notes

Since there was deep and longstanding hostility between Jews and Samaritans rooted in political and religious rivalry, a story with a Samaritan hero would have shocked a Jewish audience. The Samaritan breaks down social and ethnic barriers by serving as the friend and savior of the anonymous Jew who was waylaid on a dangerous road. Both the technique and the content are deemed to be typical of Jesus.

The lawyer's question about the greatest commandment (Luke 10:25–28) is not the original framework for the parable. Its appearance in other contexts in Mark (12:28–34) and Matthew (22:34–40) demonstrates this. Luke created the question about neighbor (Luke 10:29) to form the transition from the lawyer's question to the parable. Accordingly, the conclusion, Luke 10:36–37, is also the work of Luke, and reflects the concern of a later time.

Dishonest Steward

Luke 16:1–9

¹He also said to the disciples, "There was a rich man who had a steward, and charges were brought to him that this man was wasting his goods. ²And he called him and said to him, 'What is this that I hear about you? Turn in the account of your stewardship, for you can no longer be steward.' ³And the steward said to himself, 'What shall I do, since my master is taking the stewardship away from me? I am not strong enough to dig, and I am ashamed to beg. ⁴I have decided what to do, so that people may receive me into their houses when I am put out of the stewardship.' ⁵So, summoning his master's debtors one by one, he said to the first, 'How much do you owe my master?' ⁶He said, 'A hundred measures of oil.' And he said to him, 'Take your bill, and sit down quickly and write fifty.' ⁷Then he said to another, 'And how much do you owe?' He said, 'A hundred measures of wheat.' He said to him, 'Take your bill, and write eighty.' ⁸The master commended the dishonest steward for his shrewdness.

"For the sons of this world are more shrewd in dealing with their own generation than the sons of light. ⁹And I tell you, make friends for yourselves by means of unrighteous mammon, so that when it fails they may receive you into the eternal habitations.

¹⁰"He who is faithful in a very little is faithful also in much; and he who is dishonest in a very little is dishonest also in much. ¹¹If then you have not been faithful in the unrighteous mammon, who will entrust to you the true riches? ¹²And if you have not been faithful in that which is another's, who will give you that which is your own? ¹³No servant can serve two masters; for either he will hate the one and love the other, or he will be devoted to the one and despise the other. You cannot serve God and mammon."

Luke 16:1–8a
Luke 16:8b–9

Source: *Luke*

Notes

The Dishonest Steward embarrassed Christendom from the beginning.

The parable vividly characterizes the steward's dishonesty, and, if verse 8a belongs to the original parable, the master in the story commends him for it. Such shocking elements are typical of Jesus' authentic parables. Some Fellows, however, are convinced that verse 8a is an interpretative conclusion, not customary in Jesus' parables.

The parable has puzzled both ancient and modern interpreters. The multiple endings and explanations in verses 8b–9 and 10–13 attempt to give the parable a more orthodox interpretation by softening the commendation of the dishonest steward. These additions are clearly secondary products of later tradition.

$\mathcal{V}$ineyard Laborers   4

Matt 20:1–15

¹ "For the kingdom of heaven is like a householder who went out early in the morning to hire laborers for his vineyard. ² After agreeing with the laborers for a denarius a day, he sent them into his vineyard. ³ And going out about the third hour he saw others standing idle in the market place; ⁴ and to them he said, 'You go into the vineyard too, and whatever is right I will give you.' So they went. ⁵ Going out again about the sixth hour and the ninth hour, he did the same. ⁶ And about the eleventh hour he went out and found others standing; and he said to them, 'Why do you stand here idle all day?' ⁷ They said to him, 'Because no one has hired us.' He said to them, 'You go into the vineyard too.' ⁸ And when evening came, the owner of the vineyard said to his steward, 'Call the laborers and pay them their wages, beginning with the last, up to the first.' ⁹ And when those hired about the eleventh hour came, each of them received a denarius. ¹⁰ Now when the first came, they thought they would receive more; but each of them also received a denarius. ¹¹ And on receiving it they grumbled at the householder, ¹² saying, 'These last worked only one hour, and you have made them equal to us who have borne the burden of the day and the scorching heat.' ¹³ But he replied to one of them, 'Friend, I am doing you no wrong; did you not agree with me for a denarius? ¹⁴ Take what belongs to you, and go; I choose to give to this last as I give to you. ¹⁵ Am I not allowed to do what I choose with what belongs to me? Or do you begrudge my generosity?'

¹⁶ "So the last will be first, and the first last."

Matt 20:1–15 ▬▬▬▬▬▬ ●

Source: *Matthew*

Notes

The Vineyard Laborers exaggerates the actions of the vineyard owner: he goes into the marketplace repeatedly to hire workers for the harvest and continues the process until the eleventh hour of a twelve-hour day. When he pays everyone the same wage, it comes as a surprise to those hired early because they are paid the same wage as those hired at the end of the day, and to those hired late because they are paid a full day's wage. The upsetting and disturbing end is characteristic of the parables of Jesus.

Verse 16 is an independent saying not originally attached to the parable. The Jesus Seminar will consider it separately.

ustard Seed

Matt 13:31b–32

³¹Another parable he put before them, saying, "The kingdom of heaven is like a grain of mustard seed which a man took and sowed in his field; ³²it is the smallest of all seeds, but when it has grown it is the greatest of shrubs and becomes a tree, so that the birds of the air come and make nests in its branches."

Mark 4:31–32

³⁰And he said, "With what can we compare the kingdom of God, or what parable shall we use for it? ³¹It is like a grain of mustard seed, which, when sown upon the ground, is the smallest of all the seeds on earth; ³²yet when it is sown it grows up and becomes the greatest of all shrubs, and puts forth large branches, so that the birds of the air can make nests in its shade."

Luke 13:19

¹⁸He said therefore, "What is the kingdom of God like? And to what shall I compare it? ¹⁹It is like a grain of mustard seed which a man took and sowed in his garden; and it grew and became a tree, and the birds of the air made nests in its branches."

Thom 20:2

(20) ¹The disciples said to Jesus, "Tell us what the Kingdom of Heaven is like."

²He said to them, **"It is like a mustard seed, the smallest of all seeds. But when it falls on tilled soil, it produces a great plant and becomes a shelter for birds of the sky."**

Matt 13:31b–32	
Mark 4:31–32	
Luke 13:19	
Thom 20:2	

> *Ezekiel 17:22–23:* ²²Thus says the Lord God: "I myself will take a sprig from the lofty top of the cedar, and will set it out; I will break off from the topmost of its young twigs a tender one, and I myself will plant it upon a high and lofty mountain; ²³ on the mountain height of Israel will I plant it, that it may bring forth boughs and bear fruit, and become a noble cedar; and under it will dwell all kinds of beasts; in the shade of its branches birds of every sort will nest."

Sources: *Q, Thomas, Synoptics*

Notes

The Mustard Seed originated with Jesus because the proverbially small mustard seed is a surprising metaphor for the kingdom. In everyday usage, the proper figure for the kingdom of God is greatness, not smallness.

As the parable was handed on, interpreters converted the parable into the contrast between small beginnings (small seed) and great outcome (great tree). This process can be observed in both Mark and Thomas, where the small seed becomes a great shrub or plant; in Matthew and Luke, the shrub (plant) has actually become a tree, probably under the influence of Ezekiel 17:22–23—the great cedar representing Israel. In the hands of Jesus, the Mustard Seed is a parody of the noble cedar. Subsequent interpreters transformed the modest shrub into the traditional towering tree.

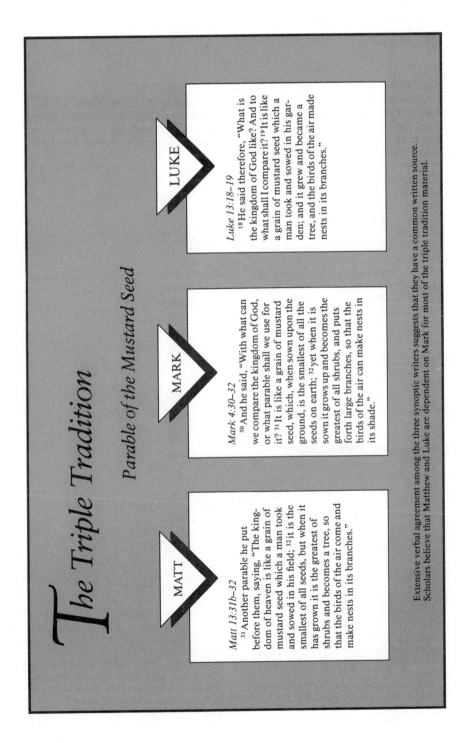

The Triple Tradition

Parable of the Mustard Seed

MATT

Matt 13:31b–32

31 Another parable he put before them, saying, "The kingdom of heaven is like a grain of mustard seed which a man took and sowed in his field; 32 it is the smallest of all seeds, but when it has grown it is the greatest of shrubs and becomes a tree, so that the birds of the air come and make nests in its branches."

MARK

Mark 4:30–32

30 And he said, "With what can we compare the kingdom of God, or what parable shall we use for it? 31 It is like a grain of mustard seed, which, when sown upon the ground, is the smallest of all the seeds on earth; 32 yet when it is sown it grows up and becomes the greatest of all shrubs, and puts forth large branches, so that the birds of the air can make nests in its shade."

LUKE

Luke 13:18–19

18 He said therefore, "What is the kingdom of God like? And to what shall I compare it? 19 It is like a grain of mustard seed which a man took and sowed in his garden; and it grew and became a tree, and the birds of the air made nests in its branches."

Extensive verbal agreement among the three synoptic writers suggests that they have a common written source. Scholars believe that Matthew and Luke are dependent on Mark for most of the triple tradition material.

Lost Coin

Luke 15:8–10

¹Now the tax collectors and sinners were all drawing near to hear him. ²And the Pharisees and the scribes murmured, saying, "This man receives sinners and eats with them."

³So he told them this parable: ⁴"What man of you, having a hundred sheep, if he has lost one of them, does not leave the ninety-nine in the wilderness, and go after the one which is lost, until he finds it? ⁵And when he has found it, he lays it on his shoulders, rejoicing. ⁶And when he comes home, he calls together his friends and his neighbors, saying to them, 'Rejoice with me, for I have found my sheep which was lost.'

⁷"Just so, I tell you, there will be more joy in heaven over one sinner who repents than over ninety-nine righteous persons who need no repentance.

⁸"Or what woman, having ten silver coins, if she loses one coin, does not light a lamp and sweep the house and seek diligently until she finds it? ⁹And when she has found it, she calls together her friends and neighbors, saying, 'Rejoice with me, for I have found the coin which I had lost.'

¹⁰"Just so, I tell you, there is joy before the angels of God over one sinner who repents."

Luke 15:8–9

Luke 15:10

Source: *Luke*

Notes

Going to great lengths to recover what was lost and then celebrating its recovery is a common theme in several authentic parables.

Luke has added verse 10, which makes the Lost Coin an exact parallel of the Lost Sheep. Luke joined the two parables together. The theme of the collection of parables in chapter 15 is repentance. As a consequence, Luke has followed the Lost Sheep and Lost Coin with the Prodigal Son, which he interprets as a "lost" son, now repentant, and thus "found."

Treasure

Matt 13:44

⁴⁴"The kingdom of heaven is like treasure hidden in a field, which a man found and covered up; then in his joy he goes and sells all that he has and buys that field."

Thom 109

(109) Jesus said, "The Kingdom is like a man who had a [hidden] treasure in his field without knowing it. And [after] he died, he left it to his son. The son did not know (about the treasure). He inherited the field and sold [it]. And the one who bought it went plowing and found the treasure. He began to lend money at interest to whomever he wished."

> R. Simeon b. Yohai taught [that the Egyptians were] like a man who inherited a piece of ground used as a dunghill. Being an indolent man he went and sold it for a trifling sum. The purchaser began working and digging it up and he found a treasure there out of which he built himself a fine palace. He began going about in public followed by a retinue of servants, all out of the treasure he found in it. When the seller saw it, he was ready to choke and exclaimed, "Alas, what have I thrown away." So when Israel was in Egypt they were set to work at bricks and mortar, and they were despised in the eyes of the Egyptians. But when the Egyptians saw them encamped under their standards by the sea in military array, they were deeply mortified and exclaimed, "Alas, what have we sent forth from our land."
> —*Midrash Rabbah*, Song of Songs 4.12.1, trans. H. Freedman and Maurice Simon (London: Soncino Press, 1939) 9:219–20.

Matt 13:44	▬▬▬▬▬ ●
Thom 109	▬▬▬▬ ●

Sources: *Matthew, Thomas*

Notes

The short, tight structure of the Treasure in Matthew is characteristic of oral tradition. The form in Thomas is more elaborate and, therefore a developed version of the parable.

By covering up the treasure and buying the field, the man deceives the original owner. This is comparable to the behavior of the Dishonest Steward (Luke 16:1–8a, §3), who swindles his master in order to provide for his own future. Surprising moves such as this appear to be characteristic of Jesus' parable technique.

Thomas' version is very similar to a rabbinic parable from *Midrash Rabbah*. Matthew's version differs markedly from this account, while the version of Thomas may have been adapted to the well-known Rabbinic tradition.

Lost Sheep

Matt 18:12–14

[10] "See that you do not despise one of these little ones; for I tell you that in heaven their angels always behold the face of my Father who is in heaven. [12] What do you think? If a man has a hundred sheep, and one of them has gone astray, does he not leave the ninety-nine on the mountains and go in search of the one that went astray? [13] And if he finds it, truly, I say to you, he rejoices over it more than over the ninety-nine that never went astray.

[14] "So it is not the will of my Father who is in heaven that one of these little ones should perish."

Matt 18:12–13		●
Matt 18:14		●
Luke 15:4–6		●
Luke 15:7		●
Thom 107		●

Luke 15:4–7

[1] Now the tax collectors and sinners were all drawing near to hear him. [2] And the Pharisees and the scribes murmured, saying, "This man receives sinners and eats with them." [3] So he told them this parable: [4] "What man of you, having a hundred sheep, if he has lost one of them, does not leave the ninety-nine in the wilderness, and go after the one which is lost, until he finds it? [5] And when he has found it, he lays it on his shoulders, rejoicing. [6] And when he comes home, he calls together his friends and his neighbors, saying to them, 'Rejoice with me, for I have found my sheep which was lost.'

[7] "Just so, I tell you, there will be more joy in heaven over one sinner who repents than over ninety-nine righteous persons who need no repentance."

Thom 107

(107) Jesus said, "The Kingdom is like a shepherd who had a hundred sheep. One of them, the largest, went astray. He left the ninety-nine and looked for that one until he found it. When he had gone to such trouble, he said to the sheep, 'I care for you more than the ninety-nine.'"

Sources: *Q, Thomas*

Notes

The shepherd who abandons ninety-nine sheep on the mountains or in the wilderness and goes in search of one stray is taking chances an ordinary shepherd would not take. Such exaggerations are typical of Jesus' parables: the man who finds the treasure buried in the field sells all he has and buys that field (§7); the merchant sells all he possesses in order to buy the single pearl of great value (§12). Never-theless, the versions of Matthew and Luke have been modified to match the emerging interests of the church in repentance and conversion (note Matt 18:14 and Luke 15:7).

The version in Thomas has moved away from the original: the lost sheep is the largest of the flock and the shepherd loves it more than the ninety-nine. These interests are alien to the authentic parables and aphorisms of Jesus.

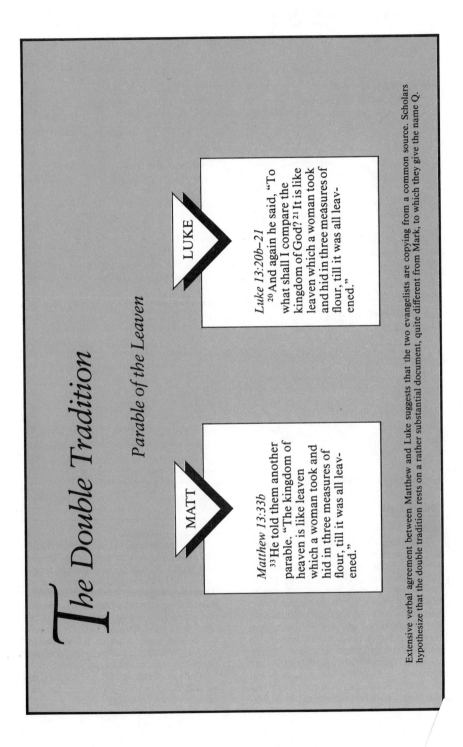

The Double Tradition

Parable of the Leaven

MATT

Matthew 13:33b
³³He told them another parable. "The kingdom of heaven is like leaven which a woman took and hid in three measures of flour, till it was all leavened."

LUKE

Luke 13:20b–21
²⁰And again he said, "To what shall I compare the kingdom of God? ²¹It is like leaven which a woman took and hid in three measures of flour, till it was all leavened."

Extensive verbal agreement between Matthew and Luke suggests that the two evangelists are copying from a common source. Scholars hypothesize that the double tradition rests on a rather substantial document, quite different from Mark, to which they give the name Q.

Luke 15:11b–32

[11] And he said, "There was a man who had two sons; [12] and the younger of them said to his father, 'Father, give me the share of property that falls to me.' And he divided his living between them. [13] Not many days later, the younger son gathered all he had and took his journey into a far country, and there he squandered his property in loose living. [14] And when he had spent everything, a great famine arose in that country, and he began to be in want. [15] So he went and joined himself to one of the citizens of that country, who sent him into his fields to feed swine. [16] And he would gladly have fed on the pods that the swine ate; and no one gave him anything. [17] But when he came to himself he said, 'How many of my father's hired servants have bread enough and to spare, but I perish here with hunger! [18] I will arise and go to my father, and I will say to him, "Father, I have sinned against heaven and before you; [19] I am no longer worthy to be called your son; treat me as one of your hired servants."' [20] And he arose and came to his father. But while he was yet at a distance, his father saw him and had compassion, and ran and embraced him and kissed him. [21] And the son said to him, 'Father, I have sinned against heaven and before you; I am no longer worthy to be called your son.' [22] But the father said to his servants, 'Bring quickly the best robe, and put it on him; and put a ring on his hand, and shoes on his feet; [23] and bring the fatted calf and kill it, and let us eat and make merry; [24] for this my son was dead, and is alive again; he was lost, and is found.' And they began to make merry.

[25] "Now his elder son was in the field; and as he came and drew near to the house, he heard music and dancing. [26] And he called one of the servants and asked what this meant. [27] And he said to him, 'Your brother has come, and your father has killed the fatted calf, because he has received him safe and sound.' [28] But he was angry and refused to go in. His father came out and entreated him, [29] but he answered his father, 'Lo, these many years I have served you, and I never disobeyed your command; yet you never gave me a kid, that I might make merry with my friends. [30] But when this son of yours came, who has devoured your living with harlots, you killed for him the fatted calf!' [31] And he said to him, 'Son, you are always with me, and all that is mine is yours. [32] It was fitting to make merry and be glad, for this your brother was dead, and is alive; he was lost, and is found.'"

Luke 15:11b–32 ▬▬▬▬ ●

Source: *Luke*

Notes

This parable is filled with extravagance and exaggeration: the younger son squanders his entire fortune on prostitutes (vs. 30) and is reduced to living with pigs; the father runs to meet him on his return, kisses and embraces him, gives him a robe and a ring, and holds a feast in his honor; the older son is angry and refuses to join the party; the father nevertheless accepts the older son and affirms his right of inheritance. Hyperbole or exaggeration—here especially in the father's excessive joy at the return of the dissolute son— is a regular and distinctive feature of Jesus' parables and aphorisms.

There are evidences, on the other hand, of Lukan composition and editing. Important Lukan themes appear, such as repentance, and Lukan stylistic features abound. There was a tendency in early interpretation to allegorize the parables: the younger son was taken to stand for the Gentiles, the older son for the Jews or Pharisees, and the father was understood as the model for God. If such allegorical traces are original, the parable cannot go back to Jesus.

While the Fellows of the Jesus Seminar were divided in their judgments, the vast majority voted red/pink.

Unjust Judge

10

Luke 18:2–8

[1] And he told them a parable, to the effect that they ought always to pray and not lose heart. [2] He said, "In a certain city there was a judge who neither feared God nor regarded man; [3] and there was a widow in that city who kept coming to him and saying, 'Vindicate me against my adversary.' [4] For a while he refused; but afterward he said to himself, 'Though I neither fear God nor regard man, [5] yet because this widow bothers me, I will vindicate her, or she will wear me out by her continual coming.'"

[6] And the Lord said, **"Hear what the unrighteous judge says. [7] And will not God vindicate his elect, who cry to him day and night? Will he delay long over them? [8] I tell you, he will vindicte them speedily. Nevertheless, when the Son of man comes, will he find faith on earth?"**

Luke 18:2–5

Luke 18:6b–8

Source: *Luke*

Notes

In the Unjust Judge, the widow's request is not granted because she is virtuous nor because her cause is just, nor is it granted because the judge is impartial and objective. Rather, she simply wears him down by her relentless coming. As in the case of the master in the Dishonest Steward (§3), the judge's response runs counter to expected behavior.

Verses 1 and 6–8 provide a secondary context, by means of which Luke links the parable to one of his special themes: prayer.

41

Feast

Matt 22:2–13

[1] And again Jesus spoke to them in parables, saying, [2] "The kingdom of heaven may be compared to a king who gave a marriage feast for his son, [3] and sent his servants to call those who were invited to the marriage feast; but they would not come. [4] Again he sent other servants, saying, 'Tell those who are invited, Behold, I have made ready my dinner, my oxen and my fat calves are killed, and everything is ready; come to the marriage feast.' [5] But they made light of it and went off, one to his farm, another to his business, [6] while the rest seized his servants, treated them shamefully, and killed them. [7] The king was angry, and he sent his troops and destroyed those murderers and burned their city. [8] Then he said to his servants, 'The wedding is ready, but those invited were not worthy. [9] Go therefore to the thoroughfares, and invite to the marriage feast as many as you find.' [10] And those servants went out into the streets and gathered all whom they found, both bad and good; so the wedding hall was filled with guests.

[11] "But when the king came in to look at the guests, he saw there a man who had no wedding garment; [12] and he said to him, 'Friend, how did you get in here without a wedding garment?' And he was speechless. [13] Then the king said to the attendants, 'Bind him hand and foot, and cast him into the outer darkness; there men will weep and gnash their teeth.'

[14] "For many are called, but few are chosen."

Luke 14:16b–24

[12] He said also to the man who had invited him, "When you give a dinner or a banquet, do not invite your friends or your brothers or your kinsmen or rich neighbors, lest they also invite you in return, and you be repaid. [13] But when you give a feast, invite the poor, the maimed, the lame, the blind, [14] and you will be blessed, because they cannot repay you. You will be repaid at the resurrection of the just."

[15] When one of those who sat at table with him heard this, he said to him, "Blessed is he who shall eat bread in the kingdom of God!" [16] But he said to him "A man once gave a great banquet, and invited many; [17] and at the time for the banquet he sent his servant to say to those who had been invited, 'Come; for all is now ready.' [18] But they all alike began to make excuses. The first said to him, 'I have bought a field, and I must go out and see it; I pray you, have me excused.' [19] And another said, 'I have bought five yoke of oxen, and I go to examine them; I pray you, have me excused.' [20] And another said, 'I have married a wife, and therefore I cannot come.' [21] So the servant came and reported this to his master. Then the householder in anger said to his servant, 'Go out quickly to the streets and lanes of the city, and bring in the poor and maimed and blind and lame.' [22] And the servant said, 'Sir, what you commanded has been done, and still there is room.' [23] And the master said to the servant, 'Go out to the highways and hedges, and compel people to come in, that my house may be filled.

[24] "'For I tell you, none of those men who were invited shall taste my banquet.'"

Thom 64:1–2

(64) [1] Jesus said, "A man had received visitors. And when he had prepared the dinner, he sent his servant to invite the guests. He went to the first one and said to him, 'My master invites you.' He said, 'I have claims against some merchants. They are coming to me this evening. I must go and give them my orders. I ask to be excused from the dinner.' He went to another and said to him, 'My master has invited you.' He said to him, 'I have just bought a house and am required for the day. I shall not have any spare time.' He went to another and said to him, 'My master invites you.' He said to him, 'My friend is going to get married, and I am to prepare the banquet. I shall not be able to come. I ask to be excused from the dinner.' He went to another and said to him, 'My master invites you.' He said to him, 'I have just bought a farm, and I am on my way to collect the rent. I shall not be able to come. I ask to be excused.' The servant returned and said to his master, 'Those whom you invited to the dinner have asked to be excused.' The master said to his servant, 'Go outside to the streets and bring back those whom you happen to meet, so that they may dine.' [2]**Businessmen and merchants will not enter the Places of My Father.**"

Matt 22:2–13		●
Luke 14:16b–23		●
Luke 14:24		●

Thom 64:1		●
Thom 64:2		●

Sources: *Q, Thomas*

Notes

In the versions of Luke and Thomas, the parable of the Feast exhibits outrageous situations typical of Jesus' parables. All parties refuse the invitation of the host, and invitations have to be issued to people of the street in order to fill the house. The parable also manifests some features of oral transmission, such as the tripling of the invitation.

Both Thomas and Luke betray signs of editing. Thomas has added an invitation to merchants to parallel his generalizing conclusion (Thom 64:2). In Luke, the first sweep of the servants to fill the hall (14:21) parallels Luke 14:13, which underscores special Lukan interest in the poor and handicapped. Verse 24 is also a Lukan addition. Luke excludes the Pharisees who reject the invitation to the (messianic) banquet.

In spite of these secondary modifications and additions, ninety percent of the Fellows of the Jesus Seminar advocated printing the versions of Luke and Thomas in pink.

The Matthean version has strayed far from the original parable. The body of the parable (22:2–10) has been turned into an allegory of the history of salvation: a king (God) prepares a feast for his son (Jesus) and invites his subjects (Israel) to the feast; they treat the invitation lightly or kill the king's servants (the prophets); the king destroys them and their city (Jerusalem) and invites others (Gentiles) to the feast. This allegory is alien to Jesus and looks back on the destruction of Jerusalem.

To this allegory Matthew has also added a warning addressed to those who enter the banquet hall but are not properly dressed: this is an allusion to Christians who enter the Christian community and then are expelled.

There is very little left of the original parable in Matthew's version.

The Earliest New Testament Gospel Fragment P⁵²

P⁵² contains a few words from John 18:31–33 and 18:37–38. This Greek fragment dates from the second century C.E., almost one hundred years after the death of Jesus. *It is reprinted with the permission of The John Rylands University Library of Manchester, England.*

*P*earl

12

Matt 13:45–46

[45] "Again, the kingdom of heaven is like a merchant in search of fine pearls, [46] who, on finding one pearl of great value, went and sold all that he had and bought it."

Thom 76:1

(76) [1] Jesus said, "The Kingdom of the Father is like a merchant who had a consignment of merchandise and who discovered a pearl. That merchant was shrewd. He sold the merchandise and bought the pearl alone for himself.

[2] "You too, seek his unfailing and enduring treasure where no moth comes near to devour and no worm destroys."

Matt 13:45–46
Thom 76:1

Sources: *Matthew, Thomas*

Notes

The Pearl is another parable independently attested by Matthew and Thomas (others are the Treasure, §7; the Planted Weeds, §25; the Fishnet, §30).

The Pearl, the Treasure, and the Fishnet all have the same form and style in Matthew; this is probably the result of Matthew's editorial activity.

The remark about the merchant's shrewdness in Thomas is probably the work of Thomas.

Differences in the two versions suggest that the original version has been modified in different directions by the two authors.

46

*P*arable of the Pearl in Thomas

The Parable of the Pearl appears on page 46, lines 14–19 of the Coptic manuscript of Thomas.
Photograph courtesy of the Institute for Antiquity and Christianity, Claremont, CA.

Mark 4:26b–29

[26] And he said, "The kingdom of God is as if a man should scatter seed upon the ground, [27] and should sleep and rise night and day, and the seed should sprout and grow, he knows not how. [28] The earth produces of itself, first the blade, then the ear, then the full grain in the ear. [29] But when the grain is ripe, at once he puts in the sickle, because the harvest has come."

Mark 4:26b–29
Thom 21:4

Thom 21:4

(21) [1] Mary said to Jesus, "Whom are Your disciples like?"

[2] He said, "They are like children who have settled in a field which is not theirs. When the owners of the field come, they will say, 'Let us have back our field.' They (will) undress in their presence in order to let them have back their field and to give it back to them. [3] Therefore I say to you, if the owner of a house knows that the thief is coming, he will begin his vigil before he comes and will not let him dig through into his house of his domain to carry away his goods. You, then, be on your guard against the world. Arm yourselves with great strength lest the robbers find a way to come to you, for the difficulty which you expect will (surely) materialize. [4] **Let there be among you a man of understanding. When the grain ripened, he came quickly with his sickle in his hand and reaped it.**

[5] "Whoever has ears to hear, let him hear."

Sources: *Mark, Thomas*

Notes

The Seed and Harvest was apparently difficult to understand from the beginning: Matthew and Luke decided to omit it from their gospels.

Thomas is acquainted with the metaphor, although the reference in Thom 21:4 can be understood simply as an allusion to Joel 3:13:

Put in the sickle,
for the harvest is ripe.
Go in, tread,
for the wine press is full.
The vats overflow,
for their wickedness is great.

Mark 4:29 has almost certainly been influenced by this passage.

The parable is tightly narrated in four steps or stages:

The farmer sows
The seed sprouts and grows
The earth produces blade, ear, and grain
The farmer reaps

The farmer acts only at the beginning and end; the seed grows secretly and the ground produces of itself. This contrast is apparently the heart of the parable.

The Fellows of the Jesus Seminar took the parable to be reminiscent of a figure of speech Jesus used, but held that it was not originally a metaphor for the kingdom. The version in Thomas is remote from the original parable.

Unmerciful Servant　　　　14

Matt 18:23–35

²¹ Then Peter came up and said to him, "Lord, how often shall my brother sin against me, and I forgive him? As many as seven times?"
²² Jesus said to him, "I do not say to you seven times, but seventy times seven.

²³ "Therefore the kingdom of heaven may be compared to a king who wished to settle accounts with his servants. ²⁴ When he began the reckoning, one was brought to him who owed him ten thousand talents; ²⁵ and as he could not pay, his lord ordered him to be sold, with his wife and children and all that he had, and payment to be made. ²⁶ So the servant fell on his knees, imploring him, 'Lord, have patience with me, and I will pay you everything.' ²⁷ And out of pity for him the lord of that servant released him and forgave him the debt. ²⁸ But that same servant, as he went out, came upon one of his fellow servants who owed him a hundred denarii; and seizing him by the throat he said, 'Pay what you owe.' ²⁹ So his fellow servant fell down and besought him, 'Have patience with me, and I will pay you.' ³⁰ He refused and went and put him in prison till he should pay the debt. ³¹ When his fellow servants saw what had taken place, they were greatly distressed, and they went and reported to their lord all that had taken place. ³² Then his lord summoned him and said to him, 'You wicked servant! I forgave you all that debt because you besought me; ³³ and should not you have had mercy on your fellow servant, as I had mercy on you?' ³⁴ And in anger his lord delivered him to the jailers, till he should pay all his debt.

³⁵ **"So also my heavenly Father will do to every one of you, if you do not forgive your brother from your heart."**

Matt 18:23–34	▬▬▬▬▬── ●
Matt 18:35	────── ●

Source: *Matthew*

Notes

The Unmerciful Servant exhibits marks of both oral tradition and exaggerations typical of Jesus' stories.

The first servant—who was probably a provincial offical—is forgiven a debt of 100 million dollars (for the sake of the comparison, we will let a denarius equal one dollar) by the king. But he is unable to forgive a fellow servant a debt of 100 dollars. The fantastic character of the parable is suggestive of the authentic parables of Jesus.

Matt 18:35 is a Matthean addition ("Heavenly Father" is a key Matthean phrase). The introduction (verses 21–22) was also provided by Matthew, although the saying in verse 22 may go back to Jesus.

Tenants

Matt 21:33b–43

33 "Hear another parable. There was a householder who planted a vineyard, and set a hedge around it, and dug a wine press in it, and built a tower, and let it out to tenants, and went into another country. 34 When the season of fruit drew near, he sent his servants to the tenants, to get his fruit; 35 and the tenants took his servants and beat one, killed another, and stoned another. 36 Again he sent other servants, more than the first; and they did the same to them. 37 Afterward he sent his son to them, saying, 'They will respect my son.' 38 But when the tenants saw the son, they said to themselves, 'This is the heir; come, let us kill him and have his inheritance.' 39 And they took him and cast him out of the vineyard, and killed him.

40 "When therefore the owner of the vineyard comes, what will he do to those tenants?" 41 They said to him, "He will put those wretches to a miserable death, and let out the vineyard to other tenants who will give him the fruits in their seasons."

42 Jesus said to them, "Have you never read in the scriptures:

'The very stone which the builders rejected
has become the head of the corner;
this was the Lord's doing,
and it is marvelous in our eyes'?

43 Therefore I tell you, the kingdom of God will be taken away from you and given to a nation producing the fruits of it."

45 When the chief priests and the Pharisees heard his parables, they perceived that he was speaking about them. 46 But when they tried to arrest him, they feared the multitudes, because they held him to be a prophet.

Mark 12:1b–11

1 And he began to speak to them in parables. "A man planted a vineyard, and set a hedge around it, and dug a pit for the wine press, and built a tower, and let it out to tenants, and went into another country. 2 When the time came, he sent a servant to the tenants, to get from them some of the fruit of the vineyard. 3 And they took him and beat him, and sent him away empty-handed. 4 Again he sent to them another servant, and they wounded him in the head, and treated him shamefully. 5 And he sent another, and him they killed; and so with many others, some they beat and some they killed. 6 He had still one other, a beloved son; finally he sent him to them, saying, 'They will respect my son.' 7 But those tenants said to one another, 'This is the heir; come, let us kill him, and the inheritance will be ours.' 8 And they took him and killed him, and cast him out of the vineyard.

9 "What will the owner of the vineyard do? He will come and destroy the tenants, and give the vineyard to others. 10 Have you not read this scripture:

'The very stone which the builders rejected
has become the head of the corner;
11 this was the Lord's doing,
and it is marvelous in our eyes'?"

12 And they tried to arrest him, but feared the multitude, for they perceived that he had told the parable against them; so they left him and went away.

Luke 20:9b–18

9 And he began to tell the people this parable: "A man planted a vineyard, and let it out to tenants, and went into another country for a long while. 10 When the time came, he sent a servant to the tenants, that they should give him some of the fruit of the vineyard; but the tenants beat him, and sent him away empty-handed. 11 And he sent another servant; him also they beat and treated shamefully, and sent him away empty-handed. 12 And he sent yet a third; this one they wounded and cast out. 13 Then the owner of the vineyard said, 'What shall I do? I will

send my beloved son; it may be they will respect him.' [14] But when the tenants saw him, they said to themselves, 'This is the heir; let us kill him, that the inheritance may be ours.' [15] And they cast him out of the vineyard and killed him.

"What then will the owner of the vineyard do to them? [16] He will come and destroy those tenants, and give the vineyard to others." When they heard this, they said, "God forbid!" [17] But he looked at them and said, "What then is this that is written:

'The very stone which the builders rejected
has become the head of the corner'?

[18] **Every one who falls on that stone will be broken to pieces; but when it falls on any one it will crush him."**

[19] The scribes and the chief priests tried to lay hands on him at that very hour, but they feared the people; for they perceived that he had told this parable against them.

Thom 65–66

(65) [1] He said, "There was a good man who owned a vineyard. He leased it to tenant farmers so that they might work it and he might collect the produce from them. He sent his servant so that the tenants might give him the produce of the vineyard. They seized his servant and beat him, all but killing him. The servant went back and told his master. The master said, 'Perhaps ⟨they⟩ did not recognize ⟨him⟩.' He sent another servant. The tenants beat this one as well. Then the owner sent his son and said, 'Perhaps they will show respect to my son.' Because the tenants knew that it was he who was the heir to the vineyard, they seized him and killed him.

[2] "Let him who has ears hear."

(66) Jesus said, **"Show me the stone which the builders have rejected. That one is the cornerstone."**

Matt 21:33b–39	▬▬▬▬▬▬▬		●
Matt 21:40–43	▬▬▬▬▬▬▬		●
Mark 12:1b–8	▬▬▬▬▬▬▬		●
Mark 12:9–11	▬▬▬▬▬▬▬		●

Luke 20:9b–15a	▬▬▬▬▬▬▬		●
Luke 20:15b–18	▬▬▬▬▬▬▬		●
Thom 65	▬▬▬▬▬▬▬		○
Thom 66	▬▬▬▬▬▬▬		●

Sources: *Synoptics, Thomas*

Notes

The Synoptic versions (Matthew, Mark, Luke) have clearly been reworked to form an allegory of the history of salvation, culminating in the rejection and death of Jesus. The landlord (God) establishes a vineyard and leases it out to tenant farmers. He sends his servants (the prophets) to the tenants to collect the rent, but they treat the servants shamefully. Finally, he sends his (beloved) son, whom the wicked tenants kill. The Christian listener knows that God has vindicated his Son by raising him from the dead, but the allegorized parable does not provide for that vindication, except indirectly in the quotation from Psalm 118:22–23 about the rejected cornerstone. The reference to the Psalm was undoubtedly added at the time the parable was allegorized.

The version in Thomas indicates that the parable once circulated without allegorical traits. Indeed, the Thomas version parallels Matthew 21:33b–39, Mark 12:1b–8, and Luke 20:9b–15a, except for the reference to the "beloved" son in Mark 12:6, and Luke 20:13. We may be confident, therefore, that Thomas is closer to the original version.

The tragic story found in Thomas portrays the realism and loss found in other parables of Jesus (for example, the Entrusted Money, §17, the Rich Farmer, §16).

Rich Farmer

Luke 12:16b–21

13 One of the multitude said to him, "Teacher, bid my brother divide the inheritance with me." 14 But he said to him, "Man, who made me a judge or divider over you?" 15 And he said to them, "Take heed, and beware of all covetousness; for a man's life does not consist in the abundance of his possessions." 16 And he told them a parable, saying, "The land of a rich man brought forth plentifully; 17 and he thought to himself, 'What shall I do, for I have nowhere to store my crops?' 18 And he said, 'I will do this: I will pull down my barns, and build larger ones; and there I will store all my grain and my goods. 19 And I will say to my soul, 'Soul, you have ample goods laid up for many years; take your ease, eat, drink, be merry.' 20 But God said to him, 'Fool! This night your soul is required of you; and the things you have prepared, whose will they be?'

21 **"So is he who lays up treasure for himself, and is not rich toward God."**

Thom 63:1

(63) 1 Jesus said, "There was a rich man who had much money. He said, 'I shall put my money to use so that I may sow, reap, plant, and fill my storehouse with produce, with the result that I shall lack nothing.' Such were his intentions, but that same night he died.

2 "Let him who has ears hear."

Luke 12:16b–20	▬▬▬▬▬ ———	●
Luke 12:21	———	●
Thom 63:1	▬▬▬▬▬ ———	●

Sources: *Luke, Thomas*

Notes

In an oral culture, the same story may be told in many different ways. Much as orchestras "perform" the same written musical score differently, the versions in Luke and Thomas are performances of the same parable. In both versions the story ends abruptly, unexpectedly: the rich man dies suddenly and there is no judgment scene. This unexpected and unelaborated ending is characteristic of the authentic parables. The less elaborate version in Thomas is probably closer to Jesus' style.

Luke has provided the narrative setting for the parable (Luke 12:13–15). Verse 15 is an independent aphorism to be considered separately. Verse 21 is an interpretative conclusion that did not go with the original parable. Thom 63:2 is also an independent saying, added now to this, now to that parable or saying (it appears 21 times in connection with words ascribed to Jesus).

How The Gospels Got Their Names

All the gospels originally circulated anonymously. Authoritative names were later assigned to them by unknown figures in the early church. In most cases, the names are guesses or perhaps the result of pious hopes.

The Gospel of Mark is attributed to John Mark, a companion of Paul (Acts 12:12, 25, 13:5, 15:36–41, Phlm 24, Col 4:10, 2 Tim 4:11), a cousin of Barnabas (Col 4:10), and perhaps an associate of Peter (1 Pet 5:13). The suggestion was first made by Papias (ca. 130 C.E.), as reported by Eusebius (d. 310), both Fathers of the ancient church. In this, as in other matters, Papias is unreliable, because he is interested in the guarantees of an eye-witness rather than in the oral process that produced Mark.

It is Papias again, as reported by Eusebius, who names Matthew (Matt 10:3) as the author of the first gospel. Matthew may have another name, Levi, which is the name given to the tax-collector in Mark 2:14 and Luke 5:23, but who is called Matthew in the parallel passage, Matt 9:9. We cannot account for the differences in name. Papias' assertion that canonical Matthew was composed in Hebrew is patently false; Matthew was composed in Greek in dependence on Q and Mark, also written in Greek by unknown authors.

The tradition that Luke the physician and companion of Paul was the author of Luke-Acts goes back to the second century C.E. The Luke in question is referred to in Col 4:14, Phlm 24, 2 Tim 4:11, where he is identified as a physician. It is improbable that the author of Luke-Acts was a physician; it is doubtful that he was a companion of Paul. Like the other attributions, this one, too, is fanciful.

The Gospel of Thomas is attributed to Didymus Judas Thomas, who was revered in the Syrian church as an apostle (Matt 10:3, Mark 3:18, Luke 6:15, Acts 1:13; cf. John 11:16, 20:24, 21:2) and as the twin brother of Jesus (so claimed by the Acts of Thomas, a third century C.E. work). The attribution to Thomas may indicate where this gospel was written, but it tells us nothing about the author.

ntrusted Money

Matt 25:14–30

14 "For it will be as when a man going on a journey called his servants and entrusted to them his property; 15 to one he gave five talents, to another two, to another one, to each according to his ability. Then he went away. 16 He who had received the five talents went at once and traded with them; and he made five talents more. 17 So also, he who had the two talents made two talents more. 18 But he who had received the one talent went and dug in the ground and hid his master's money. 19 Now after a long time the master of those servants came and settled accounts with them. 20 And he who had received the five talents came forward, bringing five talents more, saying, 'Master, you delivered to me five talents; here I have made five talents more.' 21 His master said to him, 'Well done, good and faithful servant; you have been faithful over a little, I will set you over much; **enter into the joy of your master.'** 22 And he also who had the two talents came forward, saying, 'Master, you delivered to me two talents; here I have made two talents more.' 23 His master said to him, 'Well done, good and faithful servant; you have been faithful over a little, I will set you over much; **enter into the joy of your master.'** 24 He also who had received the one talent came forward, saying, 'Master, I knew you to be a hard man, reaping where you did not sow, and gathering where you did not winnow; 25 so I was afraid, and I went and hid your talent in the ground. Here you have what is yours.' 26 But his master answered him, 'You wicked and slothful servant! You knew that I reap where I have not sowed, and gather where I have not winnowed? 27 Then you ought to have invested my money with the bankers, and at my coming I should have received what was my own with interest. 28 So take the talent from him, and give it to him who has the ten talents.

29 "**For to every one who has will more be given, and he will have abundance; but from him who has not, even what he has**

will be taken away. 30 And cast the worthless servant into the outer darkness; there men will weep and gnash their teeth.'"

Luke 19:12b–27

11 As they heard these things, he proceeded to tell a parable, because he was near to Jerusalem, and because they supposed that the kingdom of God was to appear immediately. 12 He said therefore, **"A nobleman went into a far country to receive a kingdom and then return.** 13 Calling ten of his servants, he gave them ten pounds, and said to them, 'Trade with these till I come.' 14 **But his citizens hated him and sent an embassy after him, saying, 'We do not want this man to reign over us.'** 15 When he returned, **having received the kingdom,** he commanded these servants, to whom he had given the money, to be called to him, that he might know what they had gained by trading. 16 The first came before him, saying, 'Lord, your pound has made ten pounds more.' 17 And he said to him, 'Well done, good servant! Because you have been faithful in a very little, you shall have authority **over ten cities.'** 18 And the second came, saying, 'Lord, your pound has made five pounds.' 19 And he said to him, 'And you are to be **over five cities.'** 20 Then another came, saying, 'Lord, here is your pound, which I kept laid away in a napkin; 21 for I was afraid of you, because you are a severe man; you take up what you did not lay down, and reap what you did not sow.' 22 He said to him, 'I will condemn you out of your own mouth, you wicked servant! You knew that I was a severe man, taking up what I did not lay down and reaping what I did not sow? 23 Why then did you not put my money into the bank, and at my coming I should have collected it with interest?' 24 And he said to those who stood by, 'Take the pound from him, and give it to him who has the ten pounds.' 25 (And they said to him, 'Lord, he has ten pounds!') 26 "**I tell you, that to every one who has**

will more be given; but from him who has not, even what he has will be taken away. [27] But as for these enemies of mine, who did not want me to reign over them, bring them here and slay them before me.'"

Gospel of the Nazoreans 18

(18) But since the Gospel (written) in Hebrew characters which has come into our hands enters the threat not against the man who had hid (the talent), but against him who had lived dissolutely—

for he (the master) had three servants: one who squandered his master's substance with harlots and flute-girls, one who multiplied the gain, and one who hid the talent; and accordingly one was accepted (with joy), another merely rebuked, and another cast into prison—I wonder whether in Matthew the threat which is uttered after the word against the man who did nothing may refer not to him, but by epanalepsis to the first who had feasted and drunk with the drunken. (Eusebius, *Theophania* 22 [on Matthew 25:14–15])

Matt 25:14–21b, 22–23b, 24–28
Matt 25:21c, 23c, 29–30
Luke 19:13, 15–24
Luke 19:12, 14, 25–27
GNaz 18

Source: *Q?*

Notes

The Entrusted Money has come down to us only in heavily edited form. The Matthean and Lukan versions probably reflect a form that goes back to Jesus. However, both Matthew and especially Luke have altered the story line and some details to suit their own purposes.

In a departure from normal procedures, the Fellows of the Jesus Seminar decided to print those portions of the two versions in pink that most likely go back to Jesus, and to identify with black those elements that are clearly editorial and late.

In this instance Matthew has preserved the more original form of the parable, yet even he has modified it so as to identify the returning master with Jesus at his second coming. That is made clear by the addition of the phrase, "enter into the joy of your master," after the review of the first two servants, and the insertion of "And cast the worthless servant into the outer darkness; there men will weep and gnash their teeth" after the condemnation of the third. These phrases are associated with the final judgment.

Luke has recast the parable as the story of a nobleman who petitions for a kingdom. This reflects Luke's interest in Jesus as king (Luke 1:33, 19:38, 23:3, 11, 37), who is of course rejected by the Jews (Luke 19:14). The story may be a historical reminiscence of King Archelaus, who, in 4 B.C.E., journeyed to Rome to have his rule over Judea confirmed, but was opposed by a Jewish delegation.

The generalizing conclusion (Matt 25:29, Luke 19:26) was probably added to the parable during the oral period and was thus recorded already in Q.

Luke 19:25 is a marginal note added by some scribe (readers and missionaries made their notes in the margins of handwritten manuscripts) representing an anonymous protest.

The Gospel of the Nazoreans reflects yet another version of the parable. The servants are three in number, but, in addition to the one who multiplied the money entrusted to him and the one who hid his trust, a third squanders his legacy with harlots and flute-girls. This version is almost certainly secondary.

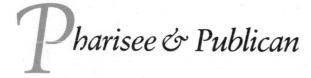

Luke 18:10–14a

⁹ He also told this parable to some who trusted in themselves that they were righteous and despised others: ¹⁰"Two men went up into the temple to pray, one a Pharisee and the other a tax collector. ¹¹ The Pharisee stood and prayed thus with himself, 'God, I thank thee that I am not like other men, extortioners, unjust, adulterers, or even like this tax collector. ¹²I fast twice a week, I give tithes of all that I get.' ¹³But the tax collector, standing far off, would not even lift up his eyes to heaven, but beat his breast, saying, 'God, be merciful to me a sinner!' ¹⁴I tell you, this man went down to his house justified rather than the other.

"For every one who exalts himself will be humbled, but he who humbles himself will be exalted."

Luke 18:10–14a

Source: *Luke*

Notes

The Pharisee and Publican portrays two ways of praying, one a public way practiced by the Pharisee, the other a private way practiced by the Publican or tax agent.

It is certain that the saying recorded in verse 14b (the reversal of the proud and the humble) is an independent adage, not originally attached to this parable.

It is unclear whether verse 14a went with the parable originally or not. If verse 14a did not belong to its original form, the parable probably simply contrasted the two ways of praying–if indeed it goes back to Jesus. If verse 14a did belong to the original import, the parable may have provocatively reversed conventional opinion about the status of the two men.

In any case, the flat characterization of the Pharisee as self-righteous and of the Publican as repentant in the framework provided by Luke belongs to the late first century, when the rivalry between Christianity and Judaism produced considerable acrimony. The Lukan interpretation allowed Christians to incorporate the parable into their anti-Jewish polemic.

Matt 13:3b–8, 18–23

¹ That same day Jesus went out of the house and sat beside the sea. ² And great crowds gathered about him, so that he got into a boat and sat there; and the whole crowd stood on the beach. ³ And he told them many things in parables, saying: "A sower went out to sow. ⁴ And as he sowed, some seeds fell along the path, and the birds came and devoured them. ⁵ Other seeds fell on rocky ground, where they had not much soil, and immediately they sprang up, since they had no depth of soil, ⁶ but when the sun rose they were scorched; and since they had no root they withered away. ⁷ Other seeds fell upon thorns, and the thorns grew up and choked them. ⁸ Other seeds fell on good soil and brought forth grain, some a hundredfold, some sixty, some thirty.

⁹ "He who has ears, let him hear."

¹⁰ Then the disciples came and said to him, "Why do you speak to them in parables?" ¹¹ And he answered them, "To you it has been given to know the secrets of the kingdom of heaven, but to them it has not been given. ¹² For to him who has will more be given, and he will have abundance; but from him who has not, even what he has will be taken away. ¹³ This is why I speak to them in parables, because seeing they do not see, and hearing they do not hear, nor do they understand. ¹⁴ With them indeed is fulfilled the prophecy of Isaiah which says:

'You shall indeed hear but never understand,
and you shall indeed see but never perceive.
¹⁵ For this people's heart has grown dull,
and their ears are heavy of hearing,
and their eyes they have closed,
lest they should perceive with their eyes,
and hear with their ears,

and understand with their heart,
and turn for me to heal them.'

¹⁶ But blessed are your eyes, for they see, and your ears, for they hear. ¹⁷ Truly, I say to you, many prophets and righteous men longed to see what you see, and did not see it, and to hear what you hear, and did not hear it.

¹⁸ "Hear then the parable of the sower. ¹⁹ When any one hears the word of the kingdom and does not understand it, the evil one comes and snatches away what is sown in his heart; this is what was sown along the path. ²⁰ As for what was sown on rocky ground, this is he who hears the word and immediately receives it with joy; ²¹ yet he has no root in himself, but endures for a while, and when tribulation or persecution arises on account of the word, immediately he falls away. ²² As for what was sown among thorns, this is he who hears the word, but the cares of the world and the delight in riches choke the word, and it proves unfruitful. ²³ As for what was sown on good soil, this is he who hears the word and understands it; he indeed bears fruit, and yields, in one case a hundredfold, in another sixty, and in another thirty."

Mark 4:3b–8, 14–20

¹ Again he began to teach beside the sea. And a very large crowd gathered about him, so that he got into a boat and sat in it on the sea; and the whole crowd was beside the sea on the land. ² And he taught them many things in parables, and in his teaching he said to them: ³ "Listen! A sower went out to sow. ⁴ And as he sowed, some seed fell along the path, and the birds came and devoured it. ⁵ Other seed fell on rocky ground, where it had not much soil, and immediately it sprang up, since it had

Sower

continued from page 57

no depth of soil; ⁶ and when the sun rose it was scorched, and since it had no root it withered away. ⁷ Other seed fell among thorns and the thorns grew up and choked it, and it yielded no grain. ⁸ And other seeds fell into good soil and brought forth grain, growing up and increasing and yielding thirtyfold and sixtyfold and a hundredfold."

⁹ And he said, "He who has ears to hear, let him hear."

¹⁰ And when he was alone, those who were about him with the twelve asked him concerning the parables. ¹¹ And he said to them, "To you has been given the secret of the kingdom of God, but for those outside everything is in parables; ¹² so that they may indeed see but not perceive, and may indeed hear but not understand; lest they should turn again, and be forgiven." ¹³ And he said to them, "Do you not understand this parable? How then will you understand all the parables? ¹⁴ The sower sows the word. ¹⁵ And these are the ones along the path, where the word is sown; when they hear, Satan immediately comes and takes away the word which is sown in them. ¹⁶ And these in like manner are the ones sown upon rocky ground, who, when they hear the word, immediately receive it with joy; ¹⁷ and they have no root in themselves, but endure for a while; then, when tribulation or persecution arises on account of the word, immediately they fall away. ¹⁸ And others are the ones sown among thorns; they are those who hear the word, ¹⁹ but the cares of the world, and the delight in riches, and the desire for other things, enter in and choke the word, and it proves unfruitful. ²⁰ But those that were sown upon the good soil are the ones who hear the word and accept it and bear fruit, thirtyfold and sixtyfold and a hundredfold."

Luke 8:5–8a, 11–15

⁴ And when a great crowd came together and people from town after town came to him, he said in a parable: ⁵ "A sower went out to sow his seed; and as he sowed, some fell along the path, and was trodden under foot, and the birds of the air devoured it. ⁶ And some fell on the rock; and as it grew up, it withered away, because it had no moisture. ⁷ And some fell among thorns; and the thorns grew with it and choked it. ⁸ And some fell into good soil and grew, and yielded a hundredfold."

As he said this, he called out, "He who has ears to hear, let him hear."

⁹ And when his disciples asked him what this parable meant, ¹⁰ he said, "To you it has been given to know the secrets of the kingdom of God; but for others they are in parables, so that seeing they may not see, and hearing they may not understand. ¹¹ Now the parable is this: The seed is the word of God. ¹² The ones along the path are those who have heard; then the devil comes and takes away the word from their hearts, that they may not believe and be saved. ¹³ And the ones on the rock are those who, when they hear the word, receive it with joy; but these have no root, they believe for a while and in time of temptation fall away. ¹⁴ And as for what fell among the thorns, they are those who hear, but as they go on their way they are choked by the cares and riches and pleasures of life, and their fruit does not mature. ¹⁵ And as for that in the good soil, they are those who, hearing the word, hold it fast in an honest and good heart, and bring forth fruit with patience."

Thom 9

(9) Jesus said, "Now the sower went out, took a handful (of seeds), and scattered them. Some fell on the road; the birds came and gathered them up. Others fell on rock, did not take root in the soil, and did not produce ears. And others fell on thorns; they choked the seed(s) and worms ate them. And others fell on the good soil and produced good fruit: it bore sixty per measure and a hundred and twenty per measure."

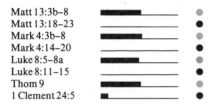

Matt 13:3b–8		
Matt 13:18–23		
Mark 4:3b–8		
Mark 4:14–20		
Luke 8:5–8a		
Luke 8:11–15		
Thom 9		
1 Clement 24:5		

1 Clement 24:5

[1]Let us consider, beloved, how the Master continually proves to us that there will be a future resurrection, of which he has made the first-fruits, by raising the Lord Jesus Christ from the dead. [2]Let us look, beloved, at the resurrection which is taking place at its proper season. [3]Day and night show us a resurrection. The night sleeps, the day arises: the day departs, night comes on. [4]Let us take the crops: how and in what way does the sowing take place? [5]**"The sower went forth" and cast each of the seeds into the ground, and they fall on to the ground, parched and bare, and suffer decay; then from their decay the greatness of the providence of the Master raises them up, and from one grain more grow and bring forth fruit.**

Sources: *Synoptics, Thomas*

Notes

Close analysis and comparison of versions of the parable reveal that all forms reflect strong editorial modification. For example, Mark probably added the note about the soil lacking depth, and Thomas probably provided the regular progress of the ending: sixty—one hundred twenty.

The allegorical interpretation (Mark 4:14–20; Matt 13:18–23; Luke 8:11–15) does not belong to the original parable, but is the product of a later time. The version in Thomas so demonstrates because it lacks allegorical traits. The allegory is ill suited to the parable and is inconsistent within itself: the seed being sown is the word, but the crop represents different classes of hearers. The possible failure of Christian preaching is a problem of the second and third generations, when the Christian community experienced differing responses to its evangelistic efforts.

Farming and harvest are common figures of speech in both Judaism and the wider Hellenistic world of the period. In Hellenistic wisdom, planting and harvest are common metaphors for education (*paideia*).

Although the Fellows of the Jesus Seminar held that no version now extant is close to what Jesus actually said, they were inclined to think that the text without allegorical traits, the version in Thomas, is closer to the original form. A significant minority wanted to print all versions in black on the grounds that the figure of the sower came into the Jesus tradition along with other common Hellenistic lore and does not necessarily represent Jesus at all.

The version in 1 Clement is a good example of the editorial modification of a parable to support a special theological point.

Mark 4:11–12 was not originally part of this unit. It will be treated with the aphorisms of Jesus.

Matt 13:9, Mark 4:9, Luke 8:8b is an independent saying, also to be considered among the aphorisms of Jesus.

# *Barren Tree*

Luke 13:6b–9

[1] There were some present at that very time who told him of the Galileans whose blood Pilate had mingled with their sacrifices. [2] And he answered them, "Do you think that these Galileans were worse sinners than all the other Galileans, because they suffered thus? [3] I tell you, No; but unless you repent you will all likewise perish. [4] Or those eighteen upon whom the tower in Siloam fell and killed them, do you think that they were worse offenders than all the others who dwelt in Jerusalem? [5] I tell you, No; but unless you repent you will all likewise perish."

[6] And he told this parable: "A man had a fig tree planted in his vineyard; and he came seeking fruit on it and found none. [7] And he said to the vinedresser, 'Lo, these three years I have come seeking fruit on this fig tree, and I find none. Cut it down; why should it use up the ground?' [8] And he answered him, 'Let it alone, sir, this year also, till I dig about it and put on manure. [9] And if it bears fruit next year, well and good; but if not, you can cut it down.'"

Luke 13:6b–9

Source: *Luke*

Notes

The fig tree is a common sign of divine blessings in Jewish lore. The parable may therefore have been drawn from a common fund of tradition and may not represent Jesus at all.

The tree in question, however, has not borne fruit for three years and is not likely to bear fruit in the future. As a consequence, the recommendation of the vinedresser to extend its life another year strikes the reader as a futile and thus exaggerated effort. This aspect of the parable convinced a majority of the Fellows of the Jesus Seminar that it originated with Jesus.

*E*mpty Jar

Thom 97

(97) Jesus said, "The Kingdom of the [Father] is like a certain woman who was carrying a jar full of meal. While she was walking [on] a road, still some distance from home, the handle of the jar broke and the meal emptied out behind her on the road. She did not realize it; she had noticed no accident. When she reached her house, she set the jar down and found it empty."

Thom 97

---

1 Kings 17:8–15: Then the word of the Lord came to him, "Arise, go to Zarephath, which belongs to Sidon, and dwell there. Behold, I have commanded a widow there to feed you." So he arose and went to Zarephath; and when he came to the gate of the city, behold, a widow was there gathering sticks; and he called to her and said, "Bring me a little water in a vessel, that I may drink." And as she was going to bring it, he called to her and said, "Bring me a morsel of bread in your hand." And she said, "As the Lord your God lives, I have nothing baked, only a handful of meal in a jar, and a little oil in a cruse; and now, I am gathering a couple of sticks, that I may go in and prepare it for myself and my son, that we may eat it, and die." And Elijah said to her, "Fear not; go and do as you have said; but first make me a little cake of it and bring it to me, and afterward make for yourself and your son. For thus says the Lord the God of Israel, 'The jar of meal shall not be spent, and the cruse of oil shall not fail, until the day that the Lord sends rain upon the earth.'" And she went and did as Elijah said; and she, and he, and her household ate for many days. The jar of meal was not spent, neither did the cruse of oil fail, according to the word of the Lord which he spoke by Elijah.

Source: *Thomas*

Notes

The structure of this parable is similar to that of the Leaven (§1). It has a surprising and provocative ending: the woman comes home with an empty rather than a full jar. A full jar would be the expected metaphor for the kingdom, so this ending is unusual.

The figure perhaps goes with Jesus' tendency to portray the kingdom as having to do with the unnoticed or unexpected or modest (cf. the Mustard Seed, §5).

The Empty Jar may be a parody of the story of Elijah and the widow of Zarephath.

*R*eturning Master

Mark 13:34–37

[32] "But of that day or that hour no one knows, not even the angels in heaven, nor the Son, but only the Father. [33] Take heed, watch; for you do not know when the time will come. [34] It is like a man going on a journey, when he leaves home and puts his servants in charge, each with his work, and commands the doorkeeper to be on watch. [35] Watch therefore—for you do not know when the master of the house will come, in the evening, or at midnight, or at cockcrow, or in the morning— [36] lest he come suddenly and find you asleep.

[37] "And what I say to you I say to all: Watch."

Luke 12:35–38

[35] "Let your loins be girded and your lamps burning, [36] and be like men who are waiting for their master to come home from the marriage feast, so that they may open to him at once when he comes and knocks. [37] Blessed are those servants whom the master finds awake when he comes; truly, I say to you, he will gird himself and have them sit at table, and he will come and serve them. [38] If he comes in the second watch, or in the third, and finds them so, blessed are those servants!

[39] "But know this, that if the householder had known at what hour the thief was coming, he would not have left his house to be broken into. [40] You also must be ready; for the Son of man is coming at an unexpected hour."

Didache 16:1a

[1] "Watch" over your life: "let your lamps" be not quenched "and your loins" be not ungirded, but be "ready," for ye know not "the hour in which our Lord cometh." [2] But be frequently gathered together seeking the things which are profitable for your souls, for the whole time of your faith shall not profit you except ye be found perfect at the last time.

Mark 13:34–36	▬▬▬▬————	◐
Mark 13:37	———————	●
Luke 12:35–38	▬▬▬▬▬———	◐
Didache 16:1a	▬▬————————	●

Sources: *Mark, Luke*

Notes

Mark and Luke at best preserve a parable fragment. The beatitude recorded in Luke 12:37 is most likely a Lukan creation. Verses 39–40 are independent sayings and will be considered separately. The allusion in Didache 16:1 is no more than that. The Returning Master may be a distant echo of a Jesus parable and is thus gray.

*A*ssassin

Thom 98

(98) Jesus said, "The Kingdom of the Father is like a certain man who wanted to kill a powerful man. In his own house he drew his sword and stuck it into the wall in order to find out whether his hand could carry through. Then he slew the powerful man."

Thom 98

Source: *Thomas*

Notes

The sheer violence and scandal of the image of the assassin suggests that it is original with Jesus. One expects a king to be violent, but not an ordinary man.

However, this image contradicts the pacific image of the kingdom customarily associated with Jesus. Furthermore, the parable echoes common wisdom—the necessary precaution a prudent man would take before encountering the village bully.

The Assassin may be a distant echo of the saying recorded in Matt 11:12: "The kingdom of heaven comes with violence and violent men attack it."

The Assassin falls on the dividing line between pink and gray with a weighted average of 1.50. Fifty percent of the Fellows voted pink, the other fifty percent voted gray/black.

Luke 16:19–31

¹⁹"There was a rich man, who was clothed in purple and fine linen and who feasted sumptuously every day. ²⁰And at his gate lay a poor man named Lazarus, full of sores, ²¹who desired to be fed with what fell from the rich man's table; moreover the dogs came and licked his sores. ²²The poor man died and was carried by the angels to Abraham's bosom. The rich man also died and was buried; ²³and in Hades, being in torment, he lifted up his eyes, and saw Abraham far off and Lazarus in his bosom. ²⁴And he called out, 'Father Abraham, have mercy upon me, and send Lazarus to dip the end of his finger in water and cool my tongue; for I am in anguish in this flame.' ²⁵But Abraham said, 'Son, remember that you in your lifetime received your good things, and Lazarus in like manner evil things; but now he is comforted here, and you are in anguish. ²⁶And besides all this, between us and you a great chasm has been fixed, in order that those who would pass from here to you may not be able, and none may cross from there to us.'

²⁷"And he said, 'Then I beg you, father, to send him to my father's house, ²⁸for I have five brothers, so that he may warn them, lest they also come into this place of torment.' ²⁹But Abraham said, 'They have Moses and the prophets; let them hear them.' ³⁰And he said, 'No, father Abraham; but if some one goes to them from the dead, they will repent.' ³¹He said to him, 'If they do not hear Moses and the prophets, neither will they be convinced if some one should rise from the dead.'"

Luke 16:19–26
Luke 16:27–31

Sources: *Luke*

Notes

The request of the rich man to send Lazarus to warn his brothers (verses 27–31) is a creation of the evangelist Luke. One of Luke's themes, which is characteristic of the early church, is Jewish lack of belief in the resurrection of Jesus. That theme is summarized well in the last line: "If they do not hear Moses and the prophets, neither will they be convinced if some one should rise from the dead" (vs. 31).

Many Fellows of the Jesus Seminar are convinced that the first part of the parable (verses 19–26) is also a Lukan creation. Luke contrasts the blessedness of the poor with the condemnation of the rich in the first beatitude and woe (Luke 6:20, 24). The bosom of Abraham is an allusion to Luke 3:8: "Do not begin to say to yourselves, 'We have Abraham as our father'; for I tell you, God is able from these stones to raise up children to Abraham." This parable, moreover, is the only one in which a character is given a proper name. And,

finally, the theme of the afterlife is widespread in folk tales in the ancient Near East. Luke has probably taken one of these common stories and refashioned it into this parable.

Other Fellows reasoned that the first half of this parable depicts a scandalous scene reminiscent of Jesus' technique in story telling. Abraham is a suitable figure for heavenly reward because he is rich and well known for his hospitality. The rich man is not censored for being rich (as Luke would have it), but for his lack of hospitality. Unlike common tales of the afterlife, this story does not have a judgment scene. Their fates are simply reversed. Such an outcome is similar to other parables of reversal (cf., for example, §4, the Vineyard Laborers, §11, the Feast).

In sum, the Fellows unanimously attribute the second part of the parable to Luke; they were divided on whether the first part is also a Lukan creation or a genuine Jesus parable.

$\mathcal{P}$lanted Weeds

Matt 13:24b–30, 37–43a

²⁴ Another parable he put before them, saying, "The kingdom of heaven may be compared to a man who sowed good seed in his field; ²⁵ but while men were sleeping, his enemy came and sowed weeds among the wheat, and went away. ²⁶ So when the plants came up and bore grain, then the weeds appeared also. ²⁷ And the servants of the householder came and said to him, 'Sir, did you not sow good seed in your field? How then has it weeds?' ²⁸ He said to them, 'An enemy has done this.' The servants said to him, 'Then do you want us to go and gather them?' ²⁹ But he said, 'No, lest in gathering the weeds you root up the wheat along with them. ³⁰ Let both grow together until the harvest; and at harvest time I will tell the reapers, Gather the weeds first and bind them in bundles to be burned, but gather the wheat into my barn.'"

. . .

³⁶ Then he left the crowds and went into the house. And his disciples came to him, saying, "Explain to us the parable of the weeds of the field." ³⁷ He answered, **"He who sows the good seed is the Son of man;** ³⁸ **the field is the world, and the good seed means the sons of the kingdom; the weeds are the** sons of the evil one, ³⁹ **and the enemy who sowed them is the devil; the harvest is the close of the age, and the reapers are angels.** ⁴⁰ **Just as the weeds are gathered and burned with fire, so will it be at the close of the age.** ⁴¹ **The Son of man will send his angels, and they will gather out of his kingdom all causes of sin and all evildoers,** ⁴² **and throw them into the furnace of fire; there men will weep and gnash their teeth.** ⁴³ **Then the righteous will shine like the sun in the kingdom of their Father.**

"He who has ears, let him hear."

Thom 57

(57) Jesus said, "The Kingdom of the Father is like a man who had [good] seed. His enemy came by night and sowed weeds among the good seed. The man did not allow them to pull up the weeds; he said to them, 'I am afraid that you will go intending to pull up the weeds and pull up the wheat along with them.' For on the day of the harvest the weeds will be plainly visible, and they will be pulled up and burned."

Matt 13:24b–30	▬▬▬_____	●
Matt 13:37–43a	_____	●
Thom 57	▬▬▬_____	●

Sources: *Matthew, Thomas*

Notes

Since the Planted Weeds is attested independently by Matthew and Thomas, it existed in oral form prior to its incorporation into these two gospels.

Matthew certainly created the allegory (Matt 13:37–43a): it reflects his notion of a mixed kingdom made up of good and evil, to be separated only at the final coming of Jesus as the Son of Man (cf. Matt 12:33–37 for another expression of this view).

The parable reflects the concern of a young Christian community to define itself over against an evil world, a concern not characteristic of Jesus. Letting the wheat and weeds grow up together suggests the final judgment rather than agricultural practice.

In the judgment of a majority of Fellows, the Planted Weeds is only distantly related to the words of Jesus, if at all.

Matt 13:43b is an independent saying frequently added to other words of Jesus. The Jesus Seminar will consider it separately.

Apocryphon of James 8:2b

[1] When we heard these things, we became distressed. [2] Now when he saw that we were distressed, he said: "This is why I say this to you (pl.), that you may know yourselves. For the Kingdom of Heaven is like an ear of grain which sprouted in a field. And when it ripened, it scattered its fruit and, in turn, filled the field with ears of grain for another year. You also: be zealous to reap for yourselves an ear of life, in order that you may be filled with the Kingdom."

ApJas 8:2b

Source: *Apocryphon of James*

Notes

The Ear of Grain is short and tightly composed like the Mustard Seed (§5). For this reason, some Fellows were attracted to its possibilities as a genuine parable of Jesus.

However, the image is extremely common in folklore of the period and the parable lacks the distinctive twist characteristic of the parables of Jesus. For these reasons, most Fellows of the Jesus Seminar took it to be a secondary increment of the Jesus tradition.

The Ear of Grain is the only parable in the Apocryphon of James that drew positive response from scholars.

Matt 25:1–13

¹ "Then the kingdom of heaven shall be compared to ten maidens who took their lamps and went to meet the bridegroom. ² Five of them were foolish, and five were wise. ³ For when the foolish took their lamps, they took no oil with them; ⁴ but the wise took flasks of oil with their lamps. ⁵ As the bridegroom was delayed, they all slumbered and slept. ⁶ But at midnight there was a cry, 'Behold, the bridegroom! Come out to meet him.' ⁷ Then all those maidens rose and trimmed their lamps. ⁸ And the foolish said to the wise, 'Give us some of your oil, for our lamps are going out.' ⁹ But the wise replied, 'Perhaps there will not be enough for us and for you; go rather to the dealers and buy for yourselves.' ¹⁰ And while they went to buy, the bridegroom came, and those who were ready went in with him to the marriage feast; and the door was shut. ¹¹ Afterward the other maidens came also, saying, 'Lord, lord, open to us.' ¹² But he replied, 'Truly, I say to you, I do not know you.'

¹³ **"Watch therefore, for you know neither the day nor the hour."**

Luke 13:25

²² He went on his way through towns and villages, teaching, and journeying toward Jerusalem. ²³ And some one said to him, "Lord, will those who are saved be few?" And he said to them, ²⁴ "Strive to enter by the narrow door; for many, I tell you, will seek to enter and will not be able. ²⁵ **When once the householder has risen up and shut the door, you will begin to stand outside and to knock at the door, saying, 'Lord, open to us.' He will answer you, 'I do not know where you come from.'** ²⁶ Then you will begin to say, 'We ate and drank in your presence, and you taught in our streets.' ²⁷ But he will say, 'I tell you, I do not know where you come from; depart from me, all you workers of iniquity!' ²⁸ There you will weep and gnash your teeth, when you see Abraham and Isaac and Jacob and all the prophets in the kingdom of God and you yourselves thrust out. ²⁹ And men will come from east and west, and from north and south, and sit at table in the kingdom of God. ³⁰ And behold, some are last who will be first, and some are first who will be last."

Matt 25:1–12
Matt 25:13
Luke 13:25

Source: *Matthew*

Notes

The Closed Door may derive from the common lore of the ancient Near East. It appears to have very few of the characteristics identified as typical of Jesus' parables. It exhibits no surprises or twists; the outcome is very predictable. Moreover, the parable is congenial to Matthew's view of the Christian community as a mixed lot, part of which is not suitable to enter into the final joy at the end of time (cf. the Planted Weeds, §25, and the Fishnet, §30).

The Fellows of the Jesus Seminar who voted for the parable as authentic did so because they thought its content matched Jesus' expectation of the kingdom's future coming.

The saying in Luke (13:25) embodies the same figure, but is woven into a different context.

Tower Builder

28

Luke 14:28–30

25 Now great multitudes accompanied him; and he turned and said to them, 26 "If any one comes to me and does not hate his own father and mother and wife and children and brothers and sisters, yes, and even his own life, he cannot be my disciple. 27 Whoever does not bear his own cross and come after me, cannot be my disciple.

28 **"For which of you, desiring to build a tower, does not first sit down and count the cost, whether he has enough to complete it? 29 Otherwise,** when he has laid a foundation, and is not able to finish, all who see it begin to mock him, 30 saying, 'This man began to build, and was not able to finish.'**

31 "Or what king, going to encounter another king in war, will not sit down first and take counsel whether he is able with ten thousand to meet him who comes against him with twenty thousand? 32 And if not, while the other is yet a great way off, he sends an embassy and asks terms of peace.

33 "So therefore, whoever of you does not renounce all that he has cannot be my disciple."

Luke 14:28–30 ▄▬▬▬▬▬ ●

Source: *Luke*

Notes

This parable, like others in the black letter category, belongs to the fund of common lore in both the Jewish and Hellenistic worlds of the time. It thus is not distinctive of Jesus.

Some Fellows of the Jesus Seminar raised the question: How do we know that a particular item was not spoken by Jesus even if it is common lore? As a sage, Jesus may have said things that were not distinctive, surprising, or shocking. The majority of the Fellows responded that the emerging Jesus tradition would more likely have functioned as a magnet, attracting stories and adages to itself, which were then attributed to Jesus, rather than Jesus borrowing items from a common fund.

68

$\mathcal{W}$arring King

Luke 14:31–33

25 Now great multitudes accompanied him; and he turned and said to them, 26 "If any one comes to me and does not hate his own father and mother and wife and children and brothers and sisters, yes, and even his own life, he cannot be my disciple. 27 Whoever does not bear his own cross and come after me, cannot be my disciple.

28 "For which of you, desiring to build a tower, does not first sit down and count the cost, whether he has enough to complete it? 29 Otherwise, when he has laid a foundation, and is not able to finish, all who see it begin to mock him, 30 saying, 'This man began to build, and was not able to finish.'

31 "Or what king, going to encounter another king in war, will not sit down first and take counsel whether he is able with ten thousand to meet him who comes against him with twenty thousand? 32 And if not, while the other is yet a great way off, he sends an embassy and asks terms of peace.

33 "So therefore, whoever of you does not renounce all that he has cannot be my disciple."

Luke 14:31–32	▬———— ●
Luke 14:33	———— ●

Source: *Luke*

Notes

The analysis of the Warring King is identical to that of the Tower Builder, §28. The two parables are customarily treated together because they are analogous. The notes on §28 are thus applicable to §29.

Luke 14:33 is an editorial comment created by Luke: the twin parables become examples of the devotion required by disciples.

ishnet

Matt 13:47–50

⁴⁷"Again, the kingdom of heaven is like a net which was thrown into the sea and gathered fish of every kind; ⁴⁸when it was full, men drew it ashore and sat down and sorted the good into vessels but threw away the bad.

⁴⁹"So it will be at the close of the age. The angels will come out and separate the evil from the righteous, ⁵⁰and throw them into the furnace of fire; there men will weep and gnash their teeth."

Thom 8:1

(8) ¹And He said, "The man is like a wise fisherman who cast his net into the sea and drew it up from the sea full of small fish. Among them the wise fisherman found a fine large fish. He threw all the small fish back into the sea and chose the large fish without difficulty.

²"Whoever has ears to hear, let him hear."

Aesop, The Fisherman and the Fish: A fisherman drew in the net which he had cast a short time before and, as luck would have it, it was full of all kinds of delectable fish. But the little ones fled to the bottom of the net and slipped out through its many meshes, whereas the big ones were caught and lay stretched out in the boat.

—*Babrius and Phaedrus*, trans. and ed. by Perry, p. 9.

Matt 13:47–48
Matt 13:49–50
Thom 8:1

Sources: *Matthew, Thomas*

Notes

The Fishnet, like the Planted Weeds (§25), reflects the necessity of the young Christian movement to mark off its social boundaries from the larger world, hence the interest in sorting out the good from the bad. The separation to take place at the close of the age (Matt 13:49–50) is a typical Matthean theme and represents the way he understood the parable.

The version in Thomas, which lacks any interest in the final judgment, contrasts the small with the large. This theme is also typical of Thomas (cf. the Leaven, §1, and the Lost Sheep, §8).

The form in Thomas is quite similar to a common Hellenistic proverb about a wise fisherman recorded by Aesop. The parable therefore probably represents common wisdom and does not go back to Jesus. Matthew has revised and interpreted it, by means of verses 49–50, to suit his interest in the last judgment. Thomas has added the contrast between small and large.

Grain of Wheat

Apocryphon of James 6:11b

[11] "Become zealous about the Word. For the Word's first characteristic is faith; the second is love; the third is works. Now from these comes life. **For the Word is like a grain of wheat. When someone sowed it, he believed in it; and when it sprouted, he loved it, because he looked (forward to) many grains in the place of one; and when he worked (it), he was saved, because he prepared it for food. Again he left (some grains) to sow.** Thus it is also possible for you (pl.) to receive for yourselves the Kingdom of Heaven: unless you receive it through knowledge, you will not be able to find it."

ApJas 6:11b   ■———————— ●

Source: *Apocryphon of James*

Notes

The Grain of Wheat exhibits some similarities to the parable of the Sower (§19). However, rather than have an allegory appended as an interpretation of the parable, the Grain of Wheat has the allegory woven into the text of the narrative itself. This technique is characteristic of later Christianity. For comparison, note the treatment of the Sower in 1 Clement (§19).

Palm Shoot

metaphore is in neg.
instead of pos.
jesus usually +

Apocryphon of James 6:8b

⁵"I first spoke with you in parables, and you did not understand. Now, in turn, I speak with you openly, and you do not perceive. But it is you who were to me a parable in parables and what is apparent in what are open.

⁶"Be zealous to be saved without being urged. Rather, be ready on your (pl.) own and, if possible, go before me. For thus the Father will love you.

⁷"Become haters of hypocrisy and evil thought. For it is thought which gives birth to hypocrisy, but hypocrisy is far from the truth.

⁸"Let not **the Kingdom of Heaven** wither away. For it **is like a date-palm ⟨shoot⟩ whose fruits dropped down around it. It put forth buds and, when they blossomed, they (i.e., the fruits) caused the productivity (of the date-palm) to dry up.** Thus it is also with the fruit which came from the single root: when it (i.e., the fruit) was ⟨picked⟩, fruits were collected by many. It was really good. Is it (not) possible now to produce the plants anew for you (sing.), (and) to find it (i.e., the Kingdom)?

⁹"⟨Since⟩ I have been glorified in this manner before this time, why do you (pl.) restrain me when I am eager to go? For after my [suffering] you have constrained me to remain with you eighteen more days (or: ⟨months⟩) for the sake of the parables. ¹⁰It sufficed for some persons ⟨to⟩ pay attention to the teaching and to understand 'The Shepherds' and 'The Seed' and 'The Building' and 'The Lamps of the Virgins' and 'The Wage of the Workers' and 'The Double Drachma' and 'The Woman.'"

ApJas 6:8b   ■————   ●

Source: *Apocryphon of James*

Notes

The parable of the Palm Shoot presents a negative example of the kingdom: this is what the kingdom is *not* like. If it were a Jesus parable, it would be the only case of a negative comparison.

The image of the date palm blooming is very common in the lore of the Hellenistic world and is used here in an ordinary and predictable sense. The parable has none of the surprise and daring associated with the Jesus parables.

Thom 21:1–2

(21) [1] Mary said to Jesus, "Whom are Your **disciples** like?"

[2] He said, "They **are like children who have settled in a field which is not theirs. When the owners of the field come, they will say, 'Let us have back our field.' They (will) undress in their presence in order to let them have back their field and to give it back to them.** [3] Therefore I say to you, if the owner of a house knows that the thief is coming, he will begin his vigil before he comes and will not let him dig through into his house of his domain to carry away his goods. You, then, be on your guard against the world. Arm yourselves with great strength lest the robbers find a way to come to you, for the difficulty which you expect will (surely) materialize. [4] Let there be among you a man of understanding. When the grain ripened, he came quickly with his sickle in his hand and reaped it. [5] Whoever has ears to hear, let him hear."

Thom 21:1–2 ■———————— ●

Source: *Thomas*

Notes

This narrative appears to be a fragment of a parable or perhaps a fable. It may have been used in a baptismal context in the Christian community. It has none of the characteristics of authentic Jesus parables. Its origin and function are obscure.

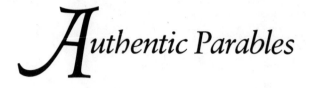 *uthentic Parables*   *Table 2*

Red Parables
5 parables, 6 versions; weighted average of 2.251 or higher

1. *Leaven*
   Matt 13:33b
   Luke 13:20b–21
2. *Good Samaritan*
   Luke 10:30b–35
3. *Dishonest Steward*
   Luke 16:1–8a

4. *Vineyard Laborers*
   Matt 20:1–15
5. *Mustard Seed*
   Thom 20:2

Pink Parables
18 parables, 28 versions; weighted average of 1.501–2.25

1. *Leaven*
   Thom 96:1
5. *Mustard Seed*
   Matt 13:31b–32
   Mark 4:31–32
   Luke 13:19
6. *Lost Coin*
   Luke 15:8–9
7. *Treasure*
   Matt 13:44
   Thom 109
8. *Lost Sheep*
   Matt 18:12–13
   Luke 15:4–6
9. *Prodigal Son*
   Luke 15:11b–32
10. *Unjust Judge*
    Luke 18:2–5
11. *Feast*
    Luke 14:16b–23
    Thom 64:1
12. *Pearl*
    Matt 13:45–46
    Thom 76:1

13. *Seed and Harvest*
    Mark 4:26b–29
14. *Unmerciful Servant*
    Matt 18:23–34
15. *Tenants*
    Thom 65
16. *Rich Farmer*
    Luke 12:16b–20
    Thom 63:1
17. *Entrusted Money*
    Matt 25:14–21b,
    22–23b, 24–28
    Luke 19:13, 15–24
18. *Pharisee and Publican*
    Luke 18:10–14a
19. *Sower*
    Matt 13:3b–8
    Mark 4:3b–8
    Thom 9
20. *Barren Tree*
    Luke 13:6b–9
21. *Empty Jar*
    Thom 97

Inauthentic Parables

Gray Parables

10 parables, 14 versions; weighted average 0.751–1.50

8. *Lost Sheep*
   Thom 107
11. *Feast*
    Matt 22:2–13
15. *Tenants*
    Matt 21:33b–39
    Mark 12:1b–8
    Luke 20:9b–15a

19. *Sower*
    Luke 8:5–8a
22. *Returning Master*
    Mark 13:34–36
    Luke 12:35–38
23. *Assassin*
    Thom 98
24. *Rich Man and Lazarus*
    Luke 16:19–26

25. *Planted Weeds*
    Matt 13:24b–30
    Thom 57
26. *Ear of Grain*
    ApJas 8:2b
27. *Closed Door*
    Matt 25:1–12

Black Parables

11 parables, 12 versions; weighted average 0.00–0.75

13. *Seed and Harvest*
    Thom 21:4
17. *Entrusted Money*
    GNaz 18
19. *Sower*
    1 Clement 24:5
22. *Returning Master*
    Didache 16:1a

27. *Closed Door*
    Luke 13:25
28. *Tower Builder*
    Luke 14:28–30
29. *Warring King*
    Luke 14:31–32

30. *Fishnet*
    Matt 13:47–48
    Thom 8:1
31. *Grain of Wheat*
    ApJas 6:11b
32. *Palm Shoot*
    ApJas 6:8b
33. *Children in the Field*
    Thom 21:1–2

Black Parable Parts

25 parts; weighted average 0.00–0.75 or by common consent

2. *Good Samaritan*
   Luke 10:36–37
3. *Dishonest Steward*
   Luke 16:8b–9
6. *Lost Coin*
   Luke 15:10
8. *Lost Sheep*
   Matt 18:14
   Luke 15:7
10. *Unjust Judge*
    Luke 18:6b–8
11. *Feast*
    Luke 14:24
    Thom 64:2

14. *Unmerciful Servant*
    Matt 18:35
15. *Tenants*
    Matt 21:40–43
    Mark 12:9–11
    Luke 20:15b–18
    Thom 66
16. *Rich Farmer*
    Luke 12:21
17. *Entrusted Money*
    Matt 25:21c, 23c, 29–30
    Luke 19:12, 14, 25–27
19. *Sower*
    Matt 13:18–23
    Mark 4:14–20
    Luke 8:11–15

22. *Returning Master*
    Mark 13:37
24. *Rich Man and Lazarus*
    Luke 16:27–31
25. *Planted Weeds*
    Matt 13:37–43a
27. *Closed Door*
    Matt 25:13
29. *Warring King*
    Luke 14:33
30. *Fishnet*
    Matt 13:49–50

The Consensus

The votes of Fellows are weighted by color. Red votes are worth 3 points, pink votes 2, gray votes 1, and black votes 0. The votes in each category are multiplied by the value, the points added, and the sum divided by the number of votes. This yields a weighted average. The weighted average determines the color in which a parable is printed.

To gain the red category a parable must achieve a weighted average in the upper fourth of the scale. That means a weighted average of 2.251 or better. Pink parables have weighted averages falling between 1.501 and 2.25. Gray parables average between 0.751 and 1.50. Black parables fall below 0.75.

Scale of Weighted Averages	
Red	2.251–3.0
Pink	1.501–2.25
Gray	0.751–1.50
Black	0.000–0.75

Weighted votes appear to be a more accurate measure of informed opinion than majorities or percentages. For example, the parable of the Prodigal Son (§9, Luke 15:11b–32) received a red vote of 48%, with an additional 31% pink. That is extraordinarily strong support. But it also received 17% black votes, with an additional 4% gray. A substantial number of Fellows were evidently convinced that the Prodigal Son, in whole or in part, is Luke's creation. As a consequence, the Prodigal is printed in pink rather than red. Its weighted average is 2.10. The strong red/pink vote in this case is slightly misleading; the weighted vote balances the red/pink vote by giving the gray/black vote some weight in the balloting, and thus better reflects the consensus.

The Fellows agreed that parables falling into either the red or pink categories would be included in the data base for determining who Jesus was. Parables designated gray or black are excluded from the data base. Authentic and inauthentic lists are provided by Tables 2 and 3.

The Consensus

There is a strong consensus at the upper end of the scale and at the lower end, as might be expected. Fellows awarded red designations to six versions of five parables, as indicated by Table 2. They excluded six parables from the data base for determining what Jesus said by designating them black. In addition, they unanimously or overwhemingly voted black on twenty-five interpretative insertions or conclusions to parables receiving other color designations. These data are detailed in Table 8.

The consensus also appears strong on weighted averages of around 2.00 and above (Table 7). Parables above this average generally drew a strong two-thirds majority of red/pink votes (Table 6). Correspondingly, the consensus is fairly strong below a weighted average of 1.00. The Closed Door (§27, Matt 25:1–12) with a weighted average of 0.93 received 70% gray/black votes. That seems fairly decisive, although the Closed Door is printed in gray.

We have to conclude that parables falling at the lower end of the pink spectrum and at the upper end of the gray range, with weighted averages between 1.00 and 2.00, received less decisive treatment. A parable like the Unmerciful Servant (§14, Matt 18:23–34) has a weighted average of 1.90, but it received 35% gray/black votes. On the other hand, 44% of the Fellows gave it a red vote. That division indicates a strong difference of judgment, which may have to do with a conclusion that raised suspicion. In any case, parables in the intermediate range invite further study and evaluation.

The Seminar achieved unanimity only on the black end of the spectrum. The parable of the Tenants (§15) received 100% black votes on the conclusion in all four versions. The conclusion incorporates the saying from Psalm 118 concerning the rejected stone (Matt 21:40–43; Mark 12:9–11; Luke 20:15b–18; Thom 66). Fellows are undivided in their judgment that this conclusion did not originate with Jesus. By unanimous consent the Fellows also excluded from the data base eighteen interpretative conclusions to parables.

At the red end of the spectrum, two versions of the Leaven (§1, Matt 13:33b, Luke 13:20b–21) attracted no black votes and received more than 60% red votes. That is very high support, indeed, considering that some Fellows are reluctant to vote red on any surviving text. The reasons given are two: (1) Jesus probably spoke Aramaic, whereas the extant records are all in Greek; (2) oral tradition does not transmit exact wording. The gray votes on the Leaven probably reflect such reservations.

Two other parables attracted no black votes. They are the Mustard Seed (§5, Mark 4:31–32, Thom 20:2) and the Pearl (§12, Thom 76:1). However, these parables garnered a lower percentage of red votes, and higher percentages of pink and gray votes, so that the weighted ranking was lower than the Leaven.

Differences in judgment should not be allowed to obscure the overall trends that emerged from the judgments of the Seminar. A positive data base of at least a dozen parables above a weighted average of 2.00 and a negative list of another dozen parables below a weighted average of 1.00 provide a firm foundation on which to erect interpetations of Jesus. This is a slightly smaller list of parables than that indicated by red/pink and gray/black categories. However, it provides a firmer foundation. This strong consensus permits scholars to tackle parables in the intermediate range, whether pink or gray, with greater confidence. The evaluations of the parables will assist materially in assessing the aphorisms, dialogues, and stories of Jesus.

Statistical Tables

Tables 4–8 provide detailed statistics.

Table 7 exhibits the absolute ranking of sixty versions of thirty-three parables by weighted vote.

Table 4 ranks the parables in descending order on the basis of percentage of red votes received. Table 5 ranks the parables in descending order on the basis of percentage of black votes received. These two tables make it easy to spot parables that received high levels of red or black votes.

Table 6 ranks the parables on the basis of combined red/pink and gray/black votes. Ranking is by percentage of red/pink in descending order, and by percentage of combined gray/black in ascending order. This table presents some interesting anomalies in relation to the table of weighted votes.

Thomas' version of the Feast (§11, 64:1) tied the Leaven for the highest combined red/pink vote. But of the 90% combined red/pink for the Feast, 62% was pink rather than red. The Leaven, on the other hand, drew 61% red and only 29% pink. This difference and the difference in gray/black vote dropped the Feast to fourteenth in the weighted ranking, while the Leaven is first.

Several parables received no black vote, as mentioned above. There was no parable that received neither black nor gray vote. However, several parables, or parts of parables, received neither red nor pink vote.

The conclusion to the Tenants, as mentioned above, received 100% black votes. The last third of the Rich Man and Lazarus (§24, Luke 16:27–31) received neither red nor pink vote. Editorial modifications of the Entrusted Money did not attract red or pink. The following received no red vote (but some pink):

§13   Seed and Harvest (Thom 21:4)
§19   Sower (1 Clem 24:5)
§23   Assassin (Thom 98)
§27   Closed Door (Matt 25:1–12, Luke 13:25)
§28   Tower Builder (Luke 14:28–30)
§29   Warring King (Luke 14:31–32)
§30   Fishnet (Matt 13:47–48, Thom 8:1)
§31   Grain of Wheat (Apocryphon of James 6:11b)

Without a single red vote and very low percentages of pink, we may be sure that we would be building on the sand in using these parables to interpret who Jesus was.

It would be equally hazardous to place any weight on the interpetative conclusions to parables which Fellows designated black by common consent.

§2   Good Samaritan (Luke 10:36–37)
§3   Dishonest Steward (Luke 16:8b–9)
§6   Lost Coin (Luke 15:10)
§8   Lost Sheep (Matt 18:14, Luke 15:7)

§10   Unjust Judge (Luke 18:6b–8)
§11   Feast (Luke 14:24, Thom 64:2)
§14   Unmerciful Servant (Matt 18:35)
§16   Rich Farmer (Luke 12:21)
§19   Sower (Matt 13:18–23, Mark 4:14–20, Luke 8:11–15)
§22   Returning Master (Mark 13:37)
§25   Planted Weeds (Matt 13:37–43a)
§27   Closed Door (Matt 25:13)
§29   Warring King (Luke 14:33)
§30   Fishnet (Matt 13:49–50)

Troublesome Cases

Three parables gave the Fellows consistent trouble. The Tenants, the Entrusted Money, and the Rich Man and Lazarus occasioned lengthy debate and were reconsidered more than once. In the end, the Fellows decided to divide the parables into parts and evaluate the parts separately.

The body of the Tenants (§15) and the Rich Man and Lazarus (§24) was separated from the corresponding conclusion. In the case of the Entrusted Montey (§17), the editorial work of either Matthew or Luke was segregated from the balance of the parable and separate votes taken. As a consequence, the Tenants without conclusion (Thom 65) made it into the pink division. Unedited versions of the Entrusted Money (Matt and Luke) also received pink designations. The remaining fragments fell into gray or black. Without the decision to separate the parts, all three parables would have been excluded from the data base. The notes on these parables provide further detail.

Parables in Thomas

Among the more interesting observations growing out of this report are those concerning the Gospel of Thomas.

Among the parables included in the red/pink category, Thomas contributed versions of nine.

Thomas' version of the Mustard Seed (§5, 20:2) received the highest weighted average (2.29), in comparison with the versions of Matt, Mark, and Luke. In this as in other instances, the Fellows adjudged the Thomas version to be closer to the original.

The Thomas version of the Feast (§11, 64:1) received the highest percentage of combined red/pink vote. Its weighted average exceeded that of Luke's version. Matthew's version did not make it into the data base.

Versions of the Pearl (§12, 76:1), the Tenants (§15, 65), and the Rich Farmer (§16, 63:1) were also ranked higher than corresponding canonical versions.

While not ranked higher than canonical versions, the Leaven (§1, 96:1), the Treasure (§7, 109), and the Sower (§19, 9) also were included in the red/pink division.

And one unique Thomas parable, the Empty Jar (§21, 97), received a pink designation by a slim margin.

Nine versions of parables found in Thomas were thus included among the thirty-four parables given a red or pink designation. That is a strong showing for a source unknown only fifty years ago.

On the other side of the ledger, the Assassin (§23, 98) and the Children in the Field (§33, 21:1–2), other parables unique to Thomas, were adjudged not to be authentic. And Thomas' versions of four canonical parables (Planted Weeds, Seed and Harvest, Fishnet, and the Lost Sheep) received gray or black designations.

Sources

Written source apparently did not play a decisive role in evaluating the parables.

Considering only parables included in the red/pink data base, seven derive from special Luke material, two from special Matthew. One is unique to Thomas. Thus, nearly half of the twenty-one parables in the category deemed to reflect the voice of Jesus to a greater or lesser extent stem from special sources.

The distribution of parables by source is detailed in on p. 82.

Three red/pink parables come from Q and Thomas, one is attested by Q, Thomas, and all three Synoptics (Mustard Seed, §5). Thomas and the Synoptics know two more parables (Tenants, §15; Sower, §19). One parable (the Entrusted Money, §17) may be derived from Q and redacted in Matthew and Luke, or Matthew and Luke may have independent sources. Four more are preserved by Thomas and one synoptic source. These eleven count for the other half of the red/pink list.

Parables falling in the gray/black group are distributed more or less evenly over all sources and combinations.

The results indicate that Fellows were rarely influenced by source, if at all.

*P*arables by Source

Multiple Source

Q & Thomas & Synoptics
  Mustard Seed (§5)

Q & Thomas
  Leaven (§1)
  Lost Sheep (§8)
  Feast (§11)

Synoptics & Thomas
  Tenants (§15)
  Sower (§19)

Mark & Thomas
  Seed and Harvest (§13)

Matthew & Thomas
  Treasure (§7)
  Pearl (§12)
  Planted Weeds (§25)
  Fishnet (§30)

Luke & Thomas
  Rich Farmer (§16)

Mark & Luke
  Returning Master (§22)

Single Source

Luke
  Good Samaritan (§2)
  Dishonest Steward (§3)
  Lost Coin (§6)
  Prodigal Son (§9)
  Unjust Judge (§10)
  Pharisee and Publican (§18)
  Barren Tree (§20)
  Rich Man and Lazarus (§24)
  Tower Builder (§28)
  Warring King (§29)

Matthew
  Vineyard Laborers (§4)
  Unmerciful Servant (§14)
  Closed Door (§27)

Thomas
  Empty Jar (§21)
  Assassin (§23)
  Children in Field (§33)

Q (or: Matthew and Luke)
  Entrusted Money (§17)

Apocryphon of James
  Ear of Grain (§26)
  Grain of Wheat (§31)
  Palm Shoot (§32)

G lossary of
Names & Terms

aphorism	a short, pithy saying usually with a sharp edge. A proverb, or maxim, or adage, reflects common sense. A proverb: "the early bird catches the worm." An aphorism: "the first shall be last, and the last first."
authentic/ inauthentic	for want of a better term, authentic refers to words that originated with Jesus, while inauthentic refers to words that originated outside of or later in the Christian tradition. The two terms unfortunately carry a value judgment that many Fellows of the Jesus Seminar do not share. Words not originating with Jesus may be as valuable as words originating with him, in the judgment of many. Yet common usage has made it difficult to use any other pair of terms.
canon	a collection or authoritative list of books accepted as holy scripture. The canon was determined for Roman Catholics at the Council of Trent in 1546 C.E.; it has never been determined for Protestants, except by common consent.
C.E. (Common Era)	now used to replace A.D. (*anno Domini*, in the year of our Lord) out of deference to those in our society who do not share the Christian way of reckoning time.
1 Clement	a letter written from Clement of Rome to the church at Corinth, about 95 C.E.
Didache	a compendium of teachings attributed to the twelve apostles. It was compiled in the early second century C.E.
double tradition	the material that Matthew and Luke have in common where Mark does not provide the middle term. Usually said to derive from a hypothetical document called Q.
Gnosticism	Gnosticism gets its name from the Greek word *gnosis* meaning knowledge or insight. For gnostics the world is divided into realms of darkness and light. The realm of darkness is the concrete world of sticks and stones, whereas the realm of light is above, completely segregated from the fallen world below.

83

Gnosis is the means of salvation for the selected few; it is the means of finding one's way back to the heavens above. Gnostic gospels therefore gravitate to Jesus' instruction as a heavenly figure.

**harmony
(of the gospels)** see synopsis

metaphor to say that A is B is metaphor. Two discrete and not entirely comparable entities are set alongside each other, juxtaposed. Distinguished from simile.

papyrus the predecessor to modern paper. Ancient books were written on the skins of animals, called parchment, or on papyrus, made from Egyptian reeds.

Q a hypothetic document on which both Matthew and Luke drew in creating their gospels; the source of the double tradition. Q gets its name from the initial letter of the German word for "source": *Quelle*.

simile to say A is like B is a simile. The less known is clarified by the better known. Distinguished from metaphor.

**Sinaiticus,
Codex** Codex Sinaiticus originally contained both the Old and New Testament, although parts of the Old Testament have been lost. The New Testament included both the Epistle of Barnabas and the Shepherd of Hermas, apparently as part of the New Testament canon.

synoptic the term means to have a common view. The synoptic gospels are those gospels that share a common view of the ministry of Jesus.

Synoptics Matthew, Mark, and Luke. So-called because they share a common view of the work and words of Jesus.

synopsis a synopsis of the gospels arranges the material in parallel columns for easy comparison. A harmony of the gospels weaves all gospel material into a single, presumably chronological strand.

tradition a body of information, customs, beliefs, stories, wisdom, and other material transmitted by word of mouth or in writing from one generation to another. The Jesus tradition is the entire body of material about Jesus being transmitted from one generation to another in the early Christian community.

triple tradition the material common to all three Synoptics, Matthew, Mark, and Luke.

**weighted
average** the value used to determine the final ranking of the parables in the polls of the Fellows of the Jesus Seminar. See p. 21 of the "Introduction" for how this value is calculated.

*P*arable Scholars:
History of Interpretation

Adolf Jülicher

The turning point of modern parable interpretation is *Die Gleichnisreden Jesu* (The Parables of Jesus), the mammoth work of Adolf Jülicher published just before the turn of the century. Jülicher dispelled the centuries-long domination of allegorical interpretation. He replaced allegory with a single point, which he argued should be of the broadest possible application. He understood that point to be a moral point, in line with the theological views associated with the great German theologian, Albrecht Ritschl, who had interpreted the Christian religion as fundamentally an ethical religion, which could be expressed as the fatherhood of God and the brotherhood of man.

C. H. Dodd

C. H. Dodd, the extremely influential British scholar, published his Shaffer Lectures given at Yale University under the title, *The Parables of the Kingdom*. This book proved to be a milestone in parable interpretation in the period between the two world wars.

Dodd accepted Jülicher's dictum that the parables of Jesus did not admit of allegorization. But he rejected Jülicher's further conclusion that the parables should be understood as teaching one point of the broadest possible moral application. Instead, he reasoned that the parables of Jesus should be interpreted in relation to the historical setting in which they were originally spoken.

Dodd's interest in the historical setting was buried, however, in his further claim that the parables of Jesus were a response to the tremendous crisis of his ministry. That crisis was the arrival of the kingdom of God. Thus Dodd did not understand Jesus as expecting a future kingdom, a cataclysmic end to history at some time in the future, but as heralding the immediate arrival of the kingdom in and through his own ministry. This view came to be called "realized *eschatology*."

Dodd's interpretation of the parables as realized eschatology did not

> *Eschatology* means last things, and refers to those events supposed to happen at the end of time. To qualify the term with "realized" suggests that the end time has already come, that it is in the process of being realized in the activities and person of Jesus.

85

win a large following. Nevertheless, his insistence that the parables should be interpreted in relation to their concrete historical setting did come to dominate parable interpretation for the next several decades.

Joachim Jeremias

Joachim Jeremias is the father of all recent parable interpretation. His book, *The Parables of Jesus,* published originally in German, has been translated into many languages and widely used as the basic work on the parables.

Jeremias accepted Dodd's contention that the parables were to be interpreted in relation to specific settings in the ministry of Jesus. Jeremias took the parables to be fundamentally apologetic in nature, that is, to be a defense of his message. They were therefore designed to correct, reprove, and attack. They were most often used in conflicts between Jesus and his critics. As a consequence, Jeremias understood the parables to contain the entire message of Jesus. His book on parables is arranged as an index to the themes in Jesus' teaching.

Perhaps the greatest contribution Jeremias made to the modern scholarly understanding of the parables was his acute sense of how the parables reflect everyday life in Palestine of the period. Jeremias grew up in Jerusalem under missionary parents and thus came to know the land and its ways then still largely untouched by the modern world. He steeped himself in ancient Jewish literature and lore and was able to bring a wealth of that knowledge to hundreds of details in the parables. For example, he points out in his book that sowing seed before planting was standard practice in ancient Palestine, so that the picture drawn by the parable of the Sower is true to common practice. It would therefore not be unusual for some seed to fall on the path worn by villagers cutting across the field, or among the thorns frequent in an unploughed field, or on rocky ground, which would occur frequently in every Palestine field. By gathering all these significant details Jeremias has put all subsequent scholars in his debt.

The Americans

Amos N. Wilder

Leadership in parable interpretation was destined to jump the Atlantic and settle in America following the second world war. Jeremias was still the master of historical detail, but the frame of reference for interpreting the parables was being provided by Amos N. Wilder, poet, literary critic, biblical scholar. He taught students and other scholars the value of poetry, of imagery, and of myth and symbol. He introduced the function of the imagination into the study of biblical and other ancient texts.

His book, *The Language of the Gospel: Early Christian Rhetoric,* was an attack on the kind of flat literalism so dominant among biblical scholars who had been trained in the historical method. The inability to appreciate the function of myth and symbol was what Wilder called a kind of "occupational cramp." Texts that were not factual were not, by definition, of great interest to such scholars. But

Wilder's call was heard and taken up by a whole company of Americans and Canadians in the 60s and 70s. Under the leadership of Wilder, parable interpretation came to be dominated by scholars working out of literary-critical canons into the aesthetics of the parable as literary form. Metaphor and symbol were soon to become the prevailing terms in speaking of parables.

Although Wilder has not written a book devoted exclusively to parables and their detail, his seminal essays, written over the years, have been collected in, *Jesus' Parables and the War of Myths*. In this book, as in his other writings, Wilder is concerned to recover the depth dimensions of imaginative and symbolic language, in which Jesus' parables and aphorisms are steeped.

Robert W. Funk

Robert W. Funk published an essay on "The Parable as Metaphor" in his book *Language, Hermeneutic, and Word of God*. This essay represented the decisive contribution to understanding metaphor as the essential element in the parables of Jesus.

As a metaphor, parable does not merely illustrate some other point, Funk argued. Rather, the parable as metaphor confronts listeners with the reality of another world. Although it draws its imagery from the world of ordinary, everyday life, parable incorporates an unexpected turn that looks through this commonplace existence to a new view of reality and actually presents that new reality to a listener as a potential to be grasped in the present. For the first time, the function of metaphor was being appreciated and applied to the parables of Jesus.

Funk also addressed for the first time the dynamic that occurs between a parable and a reader. He argued that the parable as metaphor draws the listener into it as a participant and induces the listener to make a judgment upon the situation set out in the parable and to apply that judgment to the matter at hand. Funk's interpretation of the parable of the Good Samaritan, also published in his book *Language, Hermeneutic, and Word of God,* was the first time in the history of parable interpretation that the Good Samaritan was recognized as a true parable and not an example of what it means to be a good neighbor.

Finally, Funk showed that the meaning of a parable cannot be exhausted by any one interpretation of it. A parable is open-ended in its meaning, he argued, and limited only by the general constraints of the meaning it had in its original historical and social context as determined by historical criticism. With these points firmly established, parable interpretation had come of age in America.

Dan O. Via, Jr.

Concurrently with Funk but independent of his work, Dan O. Via published his innovative work, *The Parables: Their Literary and Existential Dimensions*. Via contends that parable interpretation must move away from the narrow historical basis which Dodd and Jeremias posited as the proper context. Instead, the parables should be approached as genuine literary objects, with their own integrity, much like a work of art or a poem. The parable belongs to more than one situation, to more than the original context in which they were uttered, and should therefore be interpreted in and for a variety of contexts, like other works of art.

Both Funk and Via insisted that the parable does not have merely one point of comparison, one point at which the narrative fiction touches the subject matter. Rather, it is the parable as a whole that is the point of comparison: the kingdom is like: a woman kneading dough and putting leaven in it. The entire figure, not just the leaven, bears on the nature of the kingdom.

J. Dominic Crossan

J. Dominic Crossan grasped these emerging lines of parable interpretation and put them all together in his *In Parables: The Challenge of the Historical Jesus.* While bringing his intimate knowledge of poetry and literary criticism to bear on the parables of Jesus, he continues the principal lines of interpretation opened up by Amos Wilder and developed by Robert Funk and Dan Via. He divides the parables into three basic categories: parables of advent, parables of reversal, and parables of action. In so doing, he follows Jeremias in constructing an overview of Jesus' message out of his parables.

Funk and Crossan have been instrumental in bringing the parables of Jesus into relation with other parablers in the Western tradition. The two other great tellers of parables—there are not many in this august company—are Franz Kafka and Jorge Luis Borges. Funk's treatment of these and other relationships is to be found in his book, *Jesus As Precursor.* Crossan's comparisons are to be found in *Raid on the Articulate: Comic Eschatology in Jesus and Borges.*

American developments have broadened out into a wide stream. Students of Wilder, Funk, and Norman Perrin have played an active role in new directions. And those without particular pedigree have entered into the conversations. The Suggestions for Further Reading will provide a brief guide to the work of these precursors and successors.

Suggestions for
Further Reading

Study Instruments

The place to begin in the study of the parables and the words of Jesus generally is with the proper study instruments.

Crossan, J. Dominic, ed. *The Sayings Parallels: A Workbook for the Jesus Tradition*. Philadelphia: Fortress Press, 1986; now Sonoma, CA: Polebridge Press.

Parables and sayings attributed to Jesus are arranged in four formal categories: parables, aphorisms, dialogues, and stories. All items come from the first three centuries of the common era. Both canonical and non-canonical materials are included. Sixty versions of thirty-three parables constitute the first section of the *Workbook*.

The *Workbook* was adopted as the offical workbook of the Jesus Seminar.

Funk, Robert W., ed. *New Gospel Parallels*. 2 Vols. Philadelphia: Fortress Press, 1985; now Sonoma, CA: Polebridge Press.

These volumes provide the full context for all the sayings and parables of Jesus, including both canonical and non-canonical materials. Each gospel is presented in its own order, with parallels. It is the most advanced study instrument in English.

Kloppenborg, John S. *Q Parallels: Synopsis, Critical Notes, & Concordance*. Sonoma, CA: Polebridge Press, 1988.

This volume is valuable for the study of Q. It presents the Q texts, with all parallels, in both original languages and English translation. It includes notes to each section. *Q Parallels* gives the student some idea of what Q must have looked like.

Histories and Bibliographies

Perrin, Norman. *Jesus and the Language of the Kingdom. Symbol and Metaphor in New Testament Interpretation*. Philadelphia: Fortress Press, 1976.

Perrin provides an overview of the history of parable research, especially the developments in the U.S. and Canada.

Funk, Robert W., ed. *A Structuralist Approach to the Parables. Semeia* 1. Missoula, MT: Scholars Press, 1974.
    J. Dominic Crossan provides a basic bibliography on the parables, 236–274.

Kissinger, Warren S. *The Parables of Jesus. A History of Interpretation and Bibliography.* Metuchen, NJ: The Scarecrow Press, 1979.
    Kissinger provides both a brief history of interpretation and an exhaustive bibliography up to 1979.

Primary Studies (in chronological order)

Jülicher, Adolf. *Die Gleichnisreden Jesu* (The Parables of Jesus), Tübingen: J.C.B. Mohr, I (1888; 2d ed, 1899), II (1899); I and II reprinted 1970; two parts printed as one (Darmstadt: Wissenschaftliche Buchgesellschaft, 1963). No English translation exists.
Dodd, C. H. *The Parables of the Kingdom.* London: Nisbet & Co., 1935. 3d ed, 1936.
Jeremias, Joachim. *The Parables of Jesus.* Originally published, 1947. Revised ed, trans. S.H. Hooke. New York: Charles Scribner's Sons, 1963.
Wilder, Amos N. *The Language of the Gospel. Early Christian Rhetoric.* New York: Harper & Row, 1964. 2d ed, Cambridge, Mass.: Harvard University Press, 1971.
Wilder, Amos N. *Jesus' Parables and the War of Myths.* Ed James Breech. Philadelphia: Fortress Press, 1982.
Funk, Robert W. *Language, Hermeneutic, and Word of God. The Problem of Language in the New Testament and Contemporary Theology.* New York: Harper & Row, 1966.
Via, Dan O. *The Parables: Their Literary and Existential Dimensions.* Philadelphia: Fortress Press, 1967.
Crossan, J. Dominic. *In Parables. The Challenge of the Historical Jesus.* New York: Harper & Row, 1973.
Funk, Robert W. *Jesus As Precursor.* Missoula, MT: Scholars Press, 1975.
Crossan, J. Dominic. *The Dark Interval. Towards a Theology of Story.* Originally published 1975. 2d ed, Sonoma, CA: Polebridge Press, 1988.
Crossan, J. Dominic. *Raid on the Articulate: Comic Eschatology in Jesus and Borges.* New York: Harper & Row, 1976.
Crossan, J. Dominic. *Cliffs of Fall. Paradox and Polyvalence in the Parables of Jesus.* New York: The Seabury Press, 1980.
Funk, Robert W. *Parables and Presence. Forms of the New Testament Tradition.* Philadelphia: Fortress Press, 1982.

Additional Studies

Scott, Bernard Brandon. *Jesus, Symbol-Maker for the Kingdom.* Philadelphia: Fortress Press, 1981.
    A ground-breaking work in which the parables and aphorisms of Jesus are brought into synthesis and interpreted as symbols for the kingdom.

Breech, James. *The Silence of Jesus. The Authentic Voice of the Historical Man.* Philadelphia: Fortress Press, 1983.

A provocative and insightful work drawing on the work of Amos Wilder and literary criticism.

Scott, Bernard Brandon. "Essaying the Rock: The Authenticity of the Jesus Parable Tradition." *Forum* 2,1 (1986):3–53.

A sketch of all thirty-three parables prepared especially for the Jesus Seminar.

Cameron, Ron. "Parable and Interpretation in the Gospel of Thomas." *Forum* 2,2 (1986):3–39.

A detailed treatment of the parables unique to Thomas, prepared for the Jesus Seminar.

Scott, Bernard Brandon. *Hear Then a Parable: A Commentary on the Parables.* Philadelphia: Fortress Press, 1988.

Scott, Bernard Brandon, ed. *Parable Interpretation in America. The Shift to Language.* Sonoma, CA: Polebridge Press, 1988.

An anthology of the most important essays by the Americans who have redefined the way we look at parables.

$\mathcal{F}$ellows of
the Jesus Seminar

The Fellows of the Jesus Seminar are critical scholars. What does it mean to be a critical scholar? How can one tell a critical scholar from other kinds of scholars?

1. Critical scholars make themselves accountable to the established body of knowledge and theory. They belong to a guild of scholars, the cumulative work of which reaches back for centuries. Individual scholars may elect to add to the body of knowledge or modify particular theories, but in so doing they cannot ignore the cumulative achievements of their own fields of study. Critical scholarship forms the larger pool of learning and research that has dominated universities since the Renaissance.

2. Critical scholars adopt the critical methodologies integral to their fields of study. Biblical scholars must know and employ the methodologies of linguists since they work in foreign languages, they must know and employ the procedures of literary critics since they deal with written texts, and they must know and utilize social scientific method. And they must know other special fields of study, such as archaeology, history, philosophy, and computer science.

3. Critical scholars practice their craft by submitting their work to the judgments of peers. Untested work is not highly regarded. The first questions asked of the critical scholar is what has he or she published on the subject? And where and by whom has it been reviewed?

4. By submitting work to the judgment of other critical scholars, one is actually offering to have one's work judged by the standards and criteria common to all scholarship. This is what makes critical work critical: the acceptance and use of established standards and criteria.

5. It is precisely for this reason that critical scholarship in the biblical field does not permit special pleading on the basis of theological doctrine or other bias. Of course, critical scholars are human and subject to human frailties. The only means they have of protecting themselves against private interests is to insist that every fact, every theory, stand the test of examination by other scholars with different private interests but common standards. Scholars must make their cases on the basis of evidence accepted by all scholars.

It is therefore appropriate that Catholic scholars submit their work to the judgment of Protestants; that Christian scholars pass review by Jewish scholars; that biblical scholars measure up to the requirements of historical and philological learning in related fields. Conservative theologians may be skeptical about certain historical events (and often are). Liberal theologians may make conservative historical judgments (and often do). To cite one example, critical scholars may value secondary material in the gospels more highly than something Jesus said. For these reasons, it is difficult to guess the religious convictions or church affiliation of scholars on the basis of their critical judgments. In fundamentalism, by contrast, theology and fact are collapsed into each other, because religious conviction is the controlling element.

6. It is of course the case that scholars are alert to special biases that affect scholarly judgment on the current American scene. For example, many scholars are concerned not to perpetuate biblical translations that demean women. They see no reason to continue anti-Semitic readings of biblical texts. They prefer to avoid ethnic slurs, nationalism, and other forms of intellectual and moral provincialism. Ideally, scholars are dedicated solely to the search for truth, wherever and whenever they find it.

7. The Fellows of the Jesus Seminar, like critical scholarship generally, represent a wide spectrum of religious belief. Fellows include an ample number of both Catholics and Protestants. A few Jewish scholars have participated in the deliberations. Fellows come from all over the United States and Canada. The Seminar also has European members who have participated principally by mail. Fellows are affiliated with leading colleges, universities, and seminaries, or they are pastors of a wide variety of churches.

The scholarship represented by the Fellows belongs to the tradition of scholarship that has come to prevail in universities in Europe, Great Britain, and North America, as well as in those elsewhere in the world. It is also the scholarship that has been adopted by the predominant forms of Roman Catholicism and Protestantism; it is therefore the kind of scholarship honored in the theological seminaries connected with those churches. Even more conservative churches and their seminaries have slowly but steadily adopted the canons of critical scholarship in order to participate more fully in the research and debate characteristic of all fields of study in the modern university. Such institutions would probably move more quickly to the critical position were they not under constant attack from TV evangelists with substantial coffers. Unless biblical scholarship wants to lose its credibility—and it has come dangerously close to doing so because of its identification in the popular view with Sunday Schools and TV evangelism—it must adhere to the canons of research and publication that govern the physical sciences, the social sciences, and the humanities generally.

From the standpoint of the lay person, the scholarly process is painfully slow. Results are often minute and rarely constitute a dramatic shift in judgment. The results of the Jesus Seminar presented in this volume may appear small or even trivial to some, but they represent the fruit of decades of research and review. They lie well within the trends of all modern critical thought.

Seminar Steering Committee

Robert W. Funk, Cochair
J. Dominic Crossan, Cochair
Ron Cameron, Program Chair
Karen King, Member-at-Large

James R. Butts, Chair, Dialogues & Stories
John S. Kloppenborg, Chair, Aphorisms
John Lown, Cochair, Parables
Bernard Brandon Scott, Cochair, Parables

Fellows

James Adams
Rockville, Maryland

Prof. Robert W. Allison
Bates College

Rev. Richard L. Arthur
Zillah, Washington

Prof. Harold W. Attridge
University of Notre Dame

Prof. William Baird
Brite Divinity School
Texas Christian University

Prof. David L. Balch
Brite Divinity School
Texas Christian University

Prof. Karen Barta
Seattle University

Prof. William Beardslee
The Center for Process Studies
School of Theology at Claremont

Rev. Russell L. Bennett
Fellowship Congregational Church

Edward F. Beutner
Santa Clara University

Sterling Bjorndahl
Claremont Graduate School

Rev. John Blackwell
Mission Bell United
Methodist Church

Prof. Marcus Borg
Oregon State University

Prof. Eugene Boring
Texas Christian University

Prof. Walter E. Brooks
Sacred Heart University

Prof. Colin Brown
Fuller Theological Seminary

Prof. Dennis D. Buchholz
Great Plains Institute of Theology

Prof. James R. Butts
Westar Institute

Marvin F. Cain
Sunnyside, Washington

Prof. Ron Cameron
Wesleyan University

David Carter
Whittier, California

Prof. Bruce Chilton
Bard College

Prof. John J. Collins
University of Notre Dame

Prof. Michael Cook
Hebrew Union College

Prof. John Dominic Crossan
DePaul University

Rev. George W. Davis
Indianapolis, Indiana

Dr. Jon F. Dechow
Portola Valley, California

Prof. Arthur J. Dewey
Xavier University

Prof. Jim Dillon
University of California

Prof. James O. Duke
Pacific School of Religion

Prof. Dennis C. Duling
Canisius College

Prof. Robert T. Fortna
Vassar College

Prof. Robert W. Funk
Westar Institute

Donald J. Goergen, Ph. D.
Dominican Fathers Provincial Office

Prof. James Goss
California State University
at Northridge

Prof. William Green
University of Rochester

Prof. Heinz Guenther
Emmanuel College
Toronto School of Theology
University of Toronto

Rev. Robert G. Hamerton-Kelly
Center for International Security
and Arms Control
Stanford University

Prof. Walter Harrelson
Vanderbilt Univeristy

Prof. Charles W. Hedrick
Southwest Missouri State University

Prof. James D. Hester
University of Redlands

Prof. Julian V. Hills
Marquette University

Dr. John A. Hollar
Fortress Press

Prof. Roy W. Hoover
Whitman College

Michael Humphries
Claremont Graduate School

Prof. Arland Jacobson
Concordia College

Prof. Richard Jeske
Lutheran Theological Seminary
Philadelphia

Prof. John Kampen
Payne Theological Seminary

Prof. Perry Kea
University of Indianapolis

Prof. Chan-Hie Kim
School of Theology at Claremont

Prof. Karen King
Occidental College

Prof. John S. Kloppenborg
St. Michael's College
University of Toronto

Rev. Paul A. Kreimes
West Bloomfield, Michigan

Prof. Robert Kysar
Lutheran Theological Seminary
Philadelphia

Prof. William L. Lane
Western Kentucky University

Rev. Donald G. Love
Cole Camp, Missouri

Dr. John Lown
San Diego, California

Prof. Dennis R. MacDonald
Iliff School of Theology

Prof. A. W. Martin, Jr.
Oklahoma City University

Prof. Josephine Massyngberd-Ford
University of Notre Dame

Dr. Lee M. McDonald
Santa Clara, California

Prof. Lane C. McGaughy
Willamette University

Prof. Edgar V. McKnight
Furman University

Prof. Edward J. McMahon
Texas Christian University

Prof. Marvin W. Meyer
Chapman College

Joan W. Miller
Middletown, Connecticut

Prof. John W. Miller
Conrad Grebel College
University of Waterloo

Prof. Merrill P. Miller
Oregon State University

Prof. Robert J. Miller
Midway College

Paul Allan Mirecki
Harvard Divinity School

John William Nugent
Seattle, Washington

Prof. Rod Parrott
Disciples Seminary Foundation
School of Theology at Claremont

Stephen Patterson
Claremont Graduate School

Prof. Leo G. Perdue
Graduate Seminary
Phillips University

Bradford Price
Peninsula, Ohio

Prof. Adele Reinhartz
McMaster University

Prof. Vernon K. Robbins
Emory University

Prof. Thomas L. Robinson
Union Theological Seminary
New York

Prof. Richard L. Rohrbaugh
Lewis and Clark College

Prof. Benno Schroeder
West Germany

Prof. Bernard Brandon Scott
Graduate Seminary
Phillips University

Prof. Philip Sellew
University of Minnesota

Prof. Lou Silberman
University of Arizona

Milfred F. Smith
Orange, California

Prof. Dennis Smith
Graduate Seminary
Phillips University

Prof. Mahlon H. Smith
Rutgers University

Prof. Michael G. Steinhauser
Toronto School of Theology
University of Toronto

Prof. Robert Stoops
Western Washington University

Prof. William Stroker
Drew University

Prof. Robert Tannehill
The Methodist Theological School in
Ohio

Prof. W. Barnes Tatum
Greensboro College

Prof. Hal Taussig
Albright College and
St. Joseph's University

Prof. B. H. Throckmorton
Bangor Theological Seminary

Dr. Leif Vaage
Lima, Peru

Prof. William O. Walker, Jr.
Trinity University

Prof. John L. White
Loyola University

Prof. Amos N. Wilder, emeritus
Harvard Divinity School

*P*arables

Ranked by Red Vote

Listed by Percentages in Descending Order

	Parable	Source	R	P	G	B
1.	Leaven	Matt 13:33b	62	24	14	0
2.	Leaven	Luke 13:20b–21	61	29	10	0
3.	Good Samaritan	Luke 10:30b–35	60	29	4	7
4.	Vineyard Laborers	Matt 20:1–15	58	28	0	14
5.	Dishonest Steward	Luke 16:1–8a	52	34	7	7
6.	Prodigal Son	Luke 15:11b–32	48	31	4	17
7.	Lost Coin	Luke 15:8–9	45	41	7	7
8.	Treasure	Matt 13:44	45	28	24	3
9.	Unmerciful Servant	Matt 18:23–34	44	21	14	21
10.	Mustard Seed	Mark 4:31–32	43	36	21	0
11.	Unjust Judge	Luke 18:2–5	42	38	10	10
12.	Mustard Seed	Thom 20:2	39	50	11	0
13.	Mustard Seed	Matt 13:31b–32	38	31	24	7
14.	Mustard Seed	Luke 13:19	36	39	21	4
15.	Lost Sheep	Luke 15:4–6	32	50	14	4
16.	Pearl	Matt 13:45–46	31	45	21	3
17.	Lost Sheep	Matt 18:12–13	31	45	17	7
18.	Feast	Thom 64:1	28	62	0	10
19.	Sower	Mark 4:3b–8	28	38	3	31
20.	Sower	Matt 13:3b–8	28	38	0	34
21.	Pearl	Thom 76:1	26	52	22	0
22.	Leaven	Thom 96:1	25	50	21	4
23.	Rich Farmer	Thom 63:1	25	50	4	21
24.	Rich Farmer	Luke 12:16b–20	21	52	10	17
25.	Sower	Thom 9	21	46	0	33
26.	Sower	Luke 8:5–8a	21	43	0	36
27.	Seed and Harvest	Mark 4:26b–29	20	66	7	7
28.	Treasure	Thom 109	18	43	21	18
29.	Pharisee and Publican	Luke 18:10–14a	14	54	18	14
30.	Feast	Luke 14:16b–23	14	57	11	18
31.	Tenants	Thom 65	13	64	14	9

Table 4

Parable	Source	R	P	G	B
32. Barren Tree	Luke 13:6b–9	12	57	12	19
33. Lost Sheep	Thom 107	11	36	39	14
34. Planted Weeds	Thom 57	11	32	25	32
35. Returning Master	Mark 13:34–36	7	55	10	28
36. Planted Weeds	Matt 13:24b–30	7	29	32	32
37. Ear of Grain	ApJas 8:2b	7	28	31	34
38. Entrusted Money	Luke 19:13,15–24	4	73	19	4
39. Entrusted Money	Matt 25:14–21b, 22–23b,24–28	4	73	19	4
40. Empty Jar	Thom 97	4	64	18	14
41. Returning Master	Luke 12:35–38	4	63	11	22
42. Rich Man and Lazarus	Luke 16:19–26	4	46	21	29
43. Feast	Matt 22:2–13	4	18	32	46
44. Returning Master	Didache 16:1a	4	11	26	59
45. Palm Shoot	ApJas 6:8b	3	3	28	66
46. Children in the Field	Thom 21:1–2	3	3	8	86
47. Assassin	Thom 98	0	50	25	25
48. Closed Door	Matt 25:1–12	0	30	33	37
49. Closed Door	Luke 13:25	0	17	28	55
50. Fishnet	Thom 8:1	0	14	22	64
51. Fishnet	Matt 13:47–48	0	14	9	77
52. Seed and Harvest	Thom 21:4	0	13	40	47
53. Tower Builder	Luke 14:28–30	0	11	47	42
54. Warring King	Luke 14:31–32	0	11	47	42
55. Tenants	Matt 21:33b–39	0	9	64	27
56. Tenants	Mark 12:1b–8	0	9	64	27
57. Tenants	Luke 20:9b–15a	0	9	64	27
58. Sower	1 Clement 24:5	0	4	21	75
59. Entrusted Money	GNaz 18	0	4	17	79
60. Grain of Wheat	ApJas 6:11b	0	3	38	59

Parables

Ranked by Black Vote

Listed by Percentages in Descending Order

	Parable	Source	R	P	G	B
1.	Children in the Field	Thom 21:1–2	3	3	8	86
2.	Entrusted Money	GNaz 18	0	4	17	79
3.	Fishnet	Matt 13:47–48	0	14	9	77
4.	Sower	1 Clement 24:5	0	4	21	75
5.	Palm Shoot	ApJas 6:8b	3	3	28	66
6.	Fishnet	Thom 8:1	0	14	22	64
7.	Grain of Wheat	ApJas 6:11b	0	3	38	59
8.	Returning Master	Didache 16:1a	4	11	26	59
9.	Closed Door	Luke 13:25	0	17	28	55
10.	Seed and Harvest	Thom 21:4	0	13	40	47
11.	Feast	Matt 22:2–13	4	18	32	46
12.	Tower Builder	Luke 14:28–30	0	11	47	42
13.	Warring King	Luke 14:31–32	0	11	47	42
14.	Closed Door	Matt 25:1–12	0	30	33	37
15.	Sower	Luke 8:5–8a	21	43	0	36
16.	Ear of Grain	ApJas 8:2b	7	28	31	34
17.	Sower	Matt 13:3b–8	28	38	0	34
18.	Sower	Thom 9	21	46	0	33
19.	Planted Weeds	Matt 13:24b–30	7	29	32	32
20.	Planted Weeds	Thom 57	11	32	25	32
21.	Sower	Mark 4:3b–8	28	38	3	31
22.	Rich Man and Lazarus	Luke 16:19–26	4	46	21	29
23.	Returning Master	Mark 13:34–36	7	55	10	28
24.	Tenants	Matt 21:33b–39	0	9	64	27
25.	Tenants	Mark 12:1b–8	0	9	64	27
26.	Tenants	Luke 20:9b–15a	0	9	64	27
27.	Assassin	Thom 98	0	50	25	25
28.	Returning Master	Luke 12:35–38	4	63	11	22
29.	Unmerciful Servant	Matt 18:23–24	44	21	14	21
30.	Rich Farmer	Thom 63:1	25	50	4	21
31.	Barren Tree	Luke 13:6b–9	12	57	12	19

Table 5

	Parable	Source	R	P	G	B
32.	Treasure	Thom 109	18	43	21	18
33.	Feast	Luke 14:16b–23	14	57	11	18
34.	Rich Farmer	Luke 12:16b–20	21	52	10	17
35.	Prodigal Son	Luke 15:11b–32	48	31	4	17
36.	Lost Sheep	Thom 107	11	36	39	14
37.	Empty Jar	Thom 97	4	64	18	14
38.	Pharisee and Publican	Luke 18:10–14a	14	54	18	14
39.	Vineyard Laborers	Matt 20:1–15	58	28	0	14
40.	Unjust Judge	Luke 18:2–5	42	38	10	10
41.	Feast	Thom 64:1	28	62	0	10
42.	Tenants	Thom 65	13	64	14	9
43.	Mustard Seed	Matt 13:31b–32	38	31	24	7
44.	Lost Sheep	Matt 18:12–13	31	45	17	7
45.	Seed and Harvest	Mark 4:26b–29	20	66	7	7
46.	Lost Coin	Luke 15:8–9	45	41	7	7
47.	Dishonest Steward	Luke 16:1–8a	52	34	7	7
48.	Good Samaritan	Luke 10:30b–35	60	29	4	7
49.	Leaven	Thom 96:1	25	50	21	4
50.	Mustard Seed	Luke 13:19	36	39	21	4
51.	Entrusted Money	Matt 25:14–21b, 22–23b, 24–28	4	73	19	4
52.	Entrusted Money	Luke 19:13, 15–24	4	73	19	4
53.	Lost Sheep	Luke 15:4–6	32	50	14	4
54.	Treasure	Matt 13:44	45	28	24	3
55.	Pearl	Matt 13:45–46	31	45	21	3
56.	Pearl	Thom 76:1	26	52	22	0
57.	Mustard Seed	Mark 4:31–32	43	36	21	0
58.	Leaven	Matt 13:33b	62	24	14	0
59.	Mustard Seed	Thom 20:2	39	50	11	0
60.	Leaven	Luke 13:20b–21	61	29	10	0

Parables

Ranked by Red Plus Pink Vote

Listed by Percentages in Descending Order

	Parable	Source	R	P	G	B	R+P	G+B
1.	Leaven	Luke 13:20b–21	61	29	10	0	90	10
2.	Feast	Thom 64:1	28	62	0	10	90	10
3.	Good Samaritan	Luke 10:30b–35	60	29	4	7	89	11
4.	Mustard Seed	Thom 20:2	39	50	11	0	89	11
5.	Leaven	Matt 13:33b	62	24	14	0	86	14
6.	Vineyard Laborers	Matt 20:1–15	58	28	0	14	86	14
7.	Dishonest Steward	Luke 16:1–8a	52	34	7	7	86	14
8.	Lost Coin	Luke 15:8–9	45	41	7	7	86	14
9.	Seed and Harvest	Mark 4:26b–29	20	66	7	7	86	14
10.	Lost Sheep	Luke 15:4–6	32	50	14	4	82	28
11.	Unjust Judge	Luke 18:2–5	42	38	10	10	80	20
12.	Prodigal Son	Luke 15:11b–32	48	31	4	17	79	21
13.	Mustard Seed	Mark 4:31–32	43	36	21	0	79	21
14.	Pearl	Thom 76:1	26	52	22	0	78	22
15.	Tenants	Thom 65	13	64	14	9	77	23
16.	Entrusted Money	Matt 25:14–21b, 22–23b, 24–28	4	73	19	4	77	23
17.	Entrusted Money	Luke 19:13, 15–24	4	73	19	4	77	23
18.	Pearl	Matt 13:45–46	31	45	21	3	76	24
19.	Lost Sheep	Matt 18:12–13	31	45	17	7	76	24
20.	Mustard Seed	Luke 13:19	36	39	21	4	75	25
21.	Leaven	Thom 96:1	25	50	21	4	75	25
22.	Rich Farmer	Thom 63:1	25	50	4	21	75	25
23.	Treasure	Matt 13:44	45	28	24	3	73	27
24.	Rich Farmer	Luke 12:16b–20	21	52	10	17	73	27
25.	Feast	Luke 14:16b–23	14	57	11	18	71	29
26.	Mustard Seed	Matt 13:31b–32	38	31	24	7	69	31
27.	Barren Tree	Luke 13:6b–9	12	57	12	19	69	31
28.	Pharisee and Publican	Luke 18:10–14a	14	54	18	14	68	32
29.	Empty Jar	Thom 97	4	64	18	14	68	32
30.	Sower	Thom 9	21	46	0	33	67	33

Table 6

	Parable	*Source*	*R*	*P*	*G*	*B*	*R+P*	*G+B*
31.	Returning Master	Luke 12:35–38	4	63	11	22	67	33
32.	Sower	Mark 4:3b–8	28	38	3	31	66	34
33.	Sower	Matt 13:3b–8	28	38	0	34	66	34
34.	Unmerciful Servant	Matt 18:23–34	44	21	14	21	65	35
35.	Sower	Luke 8:5–8a	21	43	0	36	64	36
36.	Returning Master	Mark 13:34–36	7	55	10	28	62	38
37.	Treasure	Thom 109	18	43	21	18	61	39
38.	Rich Man and Lazarus	Luke 16:19–26	4	46	21	29	50	50
39.	Assassin	Thom 98	0	50	25	25	50	50
40.	Lost Sheep	Thom 107	11	36	39	14	47	53
41.	Planted Weeds	Thom 57	11	32	25	32	43	57
42.	Planted Weeds	Matt 13:24b–30	7	29	32	32	36	64
43.	Ear of Grain	ApJas 8:2b	7	28	31	34	35	65
44.	Closed Door	Matt 25:1–12	0	30	33	37	30	70
45.	Feast	Matt 22:2–13	4	18	32	46	22	78
46.	Closed Door	Luke 13:25	0	17	28	55	17	83
47.	Returning Master	Didache 16:1a	4	11	26	59	15	85
48.	Fishnet	Thom 8:1	0	14	22	64	14	86
49.	Fishnet	Matt 13:47–48	0	14	9	77	14	86
50.	Seed and Harvest	Thom 21:4	0	13	40	47	13	87
51.	Warring King	Luke 14:31–32	0	11	47	42	11	89
52.	Tower Builder	Luke 14:28–30	0	11	47	42	11	89
53.	Tenants	Matt 21:33b–39	0	9	64	27	9	91
54.	Tenants	Mark 12:1b–8	0	9	64	27	9	91
55.	Tenants	Luke 20:9b–15a	0	9	64	27	9	91
56.	Palm Shoot	ApJas 6:8b	3	3	28	66	6	94
57.	Children in the Field	Thom 21:1–2	3	3	8	86	6	94
58.	Sower	1 Clement 24:5	0	4	21	75	4	96
59.	Entrusted Money	GNaz 18	0	4	17	79	4	96
60.	Grain of Wheat	ApJas 6:11b	0	3	38	59	3	97

Parables
Ranked by Weighted Average

1.	Leaven	Luke 13:20b–21	2.50
2.	Leaven	Matt 13:33b	2.48
3.	Good Samaritan	Luke 10:30b–35	2.43
4.	Vineyard Laborers	Matt 20:1–15	2.31
5.	Dishonest Steward	Luke 16:1–8a	2.31
6.	Mustard Seed	Thom 20:2	2.29
7.	Lost Coin	Luke 15:8–9	2.24
8.	Mustard Seed	Mark 4:31–32	2.21
9.	Treasure	Matt 13:44	2.14
10.	Lost Sheep	Luke 15:4–6	2.11
11.	Prodigal Son	Luke 15:11b–32	2.10
12.	Unjust Judge	Luke 18:2–5	2.10
13.	Mustard Seed	Luke 13:19	2.07
14.	Feast	Thom 64:1	2.07
15.	Pearl	Thom 76:1	2.04
16.	Pearl	Matt 13:45–46	2.03
17.	Lost Sheep	Matt 18:12–13	2.00
18.	Mustard Seed	Matt 13:31b–32	2.00
19.	Seed and Harvest	Mark 4:26b–29	1.99
20.	Leaven	Thom 96:1	1.96
21.	Unmerciful Servant	Matt 18:23–34	1.90
22.	Tenants	Thom 65	1.82
23.	Rich Farmer	Thom 63:1	1.79
24.	Entrusted Money	Matt 25:14–21b, 22–23b, 24–28	1.77
25.	Entrusted Money	Luke 19:13, 15–24	1.77
26.	Rich Farmer	Luke 12:16b–20	1.76
27.	Pharisee and Publican	Luke 18:10–14a	1.73
28.	Feast	Luke 14:16b–23	1.68
29.	Sower	Mark 4:3b–8	1.62
30.	Barren Tree	Luke 13:6b–9	1.62
31.	Treasure	Thom 109	1.61

Table 7

32. Empty Jar	Thom 97	1.591
33. Sower	Matt 13:3b–8	1.586
34. Sower	Thom 9	1.57
35. Sower	Luke 8:5–8a	1.50
36. Returning Master	Luke 12:35–38	1.48
37. Lost Sheep	Thom 107	1.43
38. Assassin	Thom 98	1.41
39. Returning Master	Mark 13:34–36	1.41
40. Rich Man and Lazarus	Luke 16:19–26	1.25
41. Planted Weeds	Thom 57	1.21
42. Planted Weeds	Matt 13:24b–30	1.11
43. Ear of Grain	ApJas 8:2b	1.07
44. Closed Door	Matt 25:1–12	0.93
45. Tenants	Luke 20:9b–15a	0.82
46. Tenants	Mark 12:1b–8	0.82
47. Tenants	Matt 21:33b–39	0.82
48. Feast	Matt 22:2–13	0.79
49. Warring King	Luke 14:31–32	0.68
50. Tower Builder	Luke 14:28–30	0.68
51. Seed and Harvest	Thom 21:4	0.66
52. Closed Door	Luke 13:25	0.62
53. Returning Master	Didache 16:1a	0.59
54. Fishnet	Thom 8:1	0.50
55. Grain of Wheat	ApJas 6:11b	0.45
56. Palm Shoot	ApJas 6:8b	0.45
57. Fishnet	Matt 13:47–48	0.36
58. Sower	1 Clement 24:5	0.29
59. Entrusted Money	GNaz 18	0.24
60. Children in the Field	Thom 21:1–2	0.24

Parts of Parables
Considered Black

Table 8

Ranked by Weighted Average

1.	Entrusted Money	Matt 25:21c, 23c, 29–30	0.09
2.	Entrusted Money	Luke 19:12, 14, 25–27	0.09
3.	Rich Man and Lazarus	Luke 16:27–31	0.08
4.	Tenants	Thom 66	0.00
5.	Tenants	Luke 20:15b–18	0.00
6.	Tenants	Mark 12:9–11	0.00
7.	Tenants	Matt 21:40–43	0.00
8.	Good Samaritan	Luke 10:36–37	Consensus
9.	Dishonest Steward	Luke 16:8b–9	Consensus
10.	Lost Coin	Luke 15:10	Consensus
11.	Lost Sheep	Matt 18:14 Luke 15:7	Consensus
12.	Unjust Judge	Luke 18:6b–8	Consensus
13.	Feast	Luke 14:24 Thom 64:2	Consensus
14.	Unmerciful Servant	Matt 18:35	Consensus
15.	Rich Farmer	Luke 12:21	Consensus
16.	Sower	Matt 13:18–23 Mark 4:14–20 Luke 8:11–15	Consensus
17.	Returning Master	Mark 13:37	Consensus
18.	Planted Weeds	Matt 13:37–43a	Consensus
19.	Closed Door	Matt 25:13	Consensus
20.	Warring King	Luke 14:33	Consensus
21.	Fishnet	Matt 13:49–50	Consensus

Alternative Parable Names

Traditional Names	Current Names
Doorkeeper	Returning Master (§22)
Dragnet	Fishnet (§30)
Great Supper	Feast (§11)
Harvest Time	Seed and Harvest (§13)
Wicked Husbandmen	Tenants (§15)
Marriage Feast	Feast (§11)
Net	Fishnet (§30)
Pounds	Entrusted Money (§17)
Rich Fool	Rich Farmer (§16)
Seed Growing Secretly	Seed and Harvest (§13)
Seine-Net	Fishnet (§30)
Talents	Entrusted Money (§17)
Ten Maidens	Closed Door (§27)
Ten Virgins	Closed Door (§27)
Unjust Steward	Dishonest Steward (§3)
Watchman	Returning Master (§22)
Wheat and Tares	Planted Weeds (§25)
Wicked Tenants	Tenants (§15)

Colophon

Designed & composed by Polebridge Press, Sonoma, California

Printed & bound by McNaughton & Gunn, Inc., Saline, Michigan

Display lines are set in Sabon Italic with Palatino Italic Swash Capitals

Text lines are set in Times Roman